# HOLY
# COMPANIONS

# HOLY COMPANIONS

## Spiritual Practices from the Celtic Saints

Mary C. Earle • Sylvia Maddox

MOREHOUSE PUBLISHING
*A Continuum imprint*
HARRISBURG • LONDON • NEW YORK

First published in 2000 as *Praying with the Celtic Saints* by Saint Mary's Press, Christian Brothers Publications, Winona, Minnesota.

Morehouse Publishing, P.O. Box 1321, Harrisburg, PA 17105

Morehouse Publishing is a Continuum imprint.

The psalms in this book are from The Psalter in The Book of Common Prayer, copyright © 1979 by The Church Hymnal Corporation, New York.

All other scriptural quotations in this book are from the New Revised Standard Version Bible, copyright © 1989 by the Division of Christian Education of the National Council of the Churches of Christ in the United States of America. Used by permission. All rights reserved.

The quotes herein from *An Introduction to Celtic Christianity*, edited by James P. Mackey (Scotland: T & T Clark Publishers, 1989), pp. 47–48, copyright © 1989 by T & T Clark Publishing, are used with permission.

The quotes herein from *Pennant Melangell: Place of Pilgrimage,* by A. M. Allchin, are awaiting permission from publisher.

The quote herein from *Daily Readings from Prayers and Praises in the Celtic Tradition,* edited by A. M. Allchin and Esther de Waal (Springfied, IL: Templegate Publishers, 1987), p. 74, is used with permission of Templegate Publishers, the original source of the material.

Cover art: Early Celtic Stone Footpath at Skellig Island, Ireland, copyright © Michael St. Maur Shiel/CORBIS

Cover design: Wesley Hoke

Library of Congress Cataloging-in-Publication Data

Earle, Mary C.
  Holy companions : spiritual practices from the Celtic saints / by Mary
C. Earle and Sylvia Maddox.
       p. cm.
  Rev. ed. of: Praying with the Celtic saints. c2000.
  Includes bibliographical references.
  ISBN 0-8192-1993-2 (pbk.)
  1. Christian saints—Ireland. 2. Meditations. 3. Spiritual
exercises. 4. Prayer. I. Maddox, Sylvia. II. Earle, Mary C. Praying
with the Celtic saints. III. Title.
  BX4659.I7E365 2004
  274.1'0092'3916—dc22
                                        2003021764

**Printed in the United States of America**

04 05 06 07 08 09       10 9 8 7 6 5 4 3 2 1

*Information about books, poetry, retreats, and classes offered by Mary C. Earle may be found on her website, www.marycearle.org.*

For Dr. V. Nelle Bellamy
For Doug and Peter

"Earle and Maddox introduce us to the fascinating topic of Celtic spirituality through its embodiment in the particular lives of saintly men and women. In addition, they offer any reader practical assistance for a really down-to-earth way to pray. It is both an imaginative and instructive book."
—Fr. Timothy J. Joyce, OSB, author of *Celtic Christianity: A Sacred Tradition, A Vision of Hope.*

"The time I spent with this book was charmed, and I suspect that other readers will easily spend hours with it, returning to it often. Each of us will be nourished by these encounters. For we hold in our hands a work that is itself a poem, with each chapter a stanza and each page a verse made up of spirit, memory, and miracle."
—Dr. Maria Harris, author of *Proclaim Jubilee!* and *Jubilee Time*, and a descendant of Welsh and Irish ancestors.

# Contents

# Introduction

In *Holy Companions: Spiritual Practices from the Celtic Saints,* you are invited to meet eighteen new companions for the journey. Each meditation introduces one of the Celtic saints. By the end of the meditations, you will have traveled in a company of saints, many of whom may be new acquaintances. These Celtic saints are unknown to many people in this day and age, yet they have much to teach us about a way of prayer that hallows all of life's tasks and encompasses family, creation, work, sickness, travel, eternity.

Each meditation is intended to be read slowly. A variety of prayer practices are included with each meditation, more practices than ought to be undertaken at one sitting. We hope that you will pick the practice that is most suited to your particular need and interest. Use the book at an unhurried pace, taking the time to read, reflect, and pray. This is a book intended for devotional use and for spiritual practice. Therefore it is not meant to be read at one sitting. As the Celtic saints would say, these meditations are about "our walk this day with Christ." When something catches your attention, stop, reflect, pray, journal. Befriend these Celtic saints and their stories, and savor the practices as you walk with them.

The term *Celtic* refers to those lands where the spoken languages are derived from the Celtic mother tongue. Wales,

Scotland, Ireland, the Isle of Man, Brittany, and Cornwall are all countries or regions considered to have a Celtic heritage. A case can also be made for the Celtic history of northwestern Spain. For the purposes of this volume, saints from Wales, Scotland, and Ireland are introduced.

## The Age of the Saints

All these saints come from the epoch often referred to as the Dark Ages. This was a time when the Roman Empire was crumbling due to successive invasions from the tribes of northern Europe. In 410 C.E. the city of Rome was sacked. For several centuries afterward, the known governmental and ecclesial organization of most of Europe was in disarray; the structures of society did not function, warfare was rampant, and learning all but ceased.

In the meantime, on the western fringe of Europe in the lands now known as Ireland, Scotland, and Wales, saintly men and women lived as lights in a time of darkness. They established monastic centers that attracted seekers from far and wide. In those monasteries, sacred texts were laboriously copied by candlelight, thus preserving much of what would have been lost. Men and women were formed in the Christian faith and were encouraged to embody the gospel of Jesus.

In Ireland, Scotland, and Wales, the Dark Ages are known as the Age of the Saints. During the Age of the Saints, the men and women introduced in this book, along with many others, kept the flame of the gospel alive. Their faith persevered in dark times, manifested great courage and wisdom, and permeated every aspect of daily living. The saints introduced in this book lived during times of social and economic upheaval and random violence. They knew hardship, harsh conditions, and uncertainty. They also knew the value of community, soul friends, and hospitality.

These saints are so designated by the people of their respective lands. They continue to be revered and honored in the present day. In Wales, Ireland, and Scotland, they are associated with places of pilgrimage and devotion. Should you be compelled to do so, you can journey to the sites associated with each of these saints.

*Oral Tradition and the Lives of the Saints*

The saints introduced in this book lived from the fourth to the seventh centuries, and the stories of their lives have been preserved through the oral traditions of their native lands. Few of the saints are known to have left substantial writings, and in some instances the story of a saint's life was not written down until many centuries after her or his death. Therefore the words of the saints quoted in these meditations are often the words that come to us through the oral traditions rather than from direct writings. The oral traditions, it should be noted, are living traditions, honored and cherished in their homelands. For example, Saint David of Wales is still seen as walking with the people of his country, encouraging and teaching them.

It is worth remembering as well that in oral cultures the world over, faith and wisdom are preserved through the passing down of stories from one generation to the next. Through these stories the identity of the people is shaped. The lives of the saints carry the message of these stories: how to live in Christ.

Oral tradition tends to be very conservative; it conserves what is true for faithful living, what is worth keeping. Just as Saint Paul tells us that he is handing on what he has received concerning Christ crucified, so we hand on what we have received from the traditions of Wales, Ireland, and Scotland concerning the words attributed to these saints.

Many of the elements in the lives of these saints may seem embellished or legendary. Hagiography (biographies of the saints) is often layered with tales of wonder and miracle. Benedicta Ward, scholar and author, observes that hagiography is not biography or history but the disclosure of the holiness of a particular person, "A hagiography is above all pragmatic, practical: it shows one of that great cloud of witnesses in the detail of his life on earth as he walked in the footsteps of the Man of Galilee" (p. 2). Our aim has been to see the more wondrous and miraculous parts of each saint's story as sacramental—in other words, as something pointing us to the life of Christ appearing in human life. We have hoped to discern the deeper structure and dynamic in these stories and to invite readers to see the life of Christ as lived in the life of the saint. We also hope that readers will be inspired to look for Christ's life in their own daily living.

*The* Carmina Gadelica

Most of these meditations open with a prayer drawn from the *Carmina Gadelica*. This work is an anthology of prayers from the Scottish Highlands and islands, gathered toward the end of the nineteenth century by a Scotsman named Alexander Carmichael. We owe Carmichael a great debt, for he carefully collected these living examples of oral tradition, these prayers that had been handed down from mother to daughter, from father to son for generations. This collection reveals the heart of the particular expressions of Christian faith that come from these cultures. Carmichael asked permission to record the prayers from the fishermen and weavers, the farmers and herders. He heard the living faith of a people as he transcribed the prayers. As we read these prayers today, we join in the prayer of the peoples of the living and ancient Celtic cultures, prayer that continues to this day and is still associated with saints from so long ago.

## The Faith of the Celtic Church

The faith of the Celtic saints is the faith of the Christian church. No one knows precisely when and how the Christian faith came to Britain. We do know that when Augustine arrived at Canterbury in 597, sent from Rome to become the first bishop of that city, he encountered a well-established and thriving native church. Archaeological evidence indicates that Christians were among the members of the Roman legions and citizenry who made their home in Britain. Those early Christians, who may have come to Britain as early as the second or third century, spread the faith particularly in the small urban centers that had developed with the Romans' arrival. When the legions departed to protect Rome in the early fifth century, the eastern coast of Britain became vulnerable to invasions by tribes from the continent. The resident population, many of its members Christian, was pushed to the west and out of the small urban areas. Consequently the cultures of Wales, Scotland, and Ireland influenced aspects of Christian faith and life, enriching our understanding and practice today. These lands also became home to an expression of the faith that hearkens back to a time when the church was still one. When we pray with the Celtic saints, we reach back to a church not yet split by the divisions of Rome and Constantinople, by the many denominations we know today.

*The Three in One and the One in Three*

The Celtic Christian tradition is explicitly and emphatically trinitarian. Prayers are offered to "the Three in One and the One in Three." The Trinity is named as the Three of my love. Rather than approaching the mystery of the Trinity through abstraction and doctrine, the Celtic church names the Holy Three and calls on Father, Son, and Holy Spirit in every moment of life. "The Three that seek my heart" are with us because they are eternally with one another; there is no separation or division. The Holy Trinity is known and loved as living presence, tender and majestic, merciful and powerful. In a homely way, the Celtic church knew the three Persons of the Trinity as familial. The Holy Three are ever present, ever caring, ever accompanying.

The trinitarian address found in the prayers from the *Carmina Gadelica* may seem strange at first. One has a sense of the Trinity being close at hand, immediate, and responsive. This way of praying with the Trinity leads us to see our life within that eternally loving relationship of the Three in One and the One in Three. The Holy Three become living presence.

*The Christ of My Love*

The Celtic Christian tradition emphasizes the Incarnation. Because the pre-Christian culture of these lands emphasized the divine presence in the world, the transition to an incarnational faith rooted in the gospel of Jesus Christ proved less problematic than for other cultures. The earlier religion was accustomed to seeing the divine presence in all creation. When Christianity came to these lands, the name of Jesus Christ was given to the incarnate reality already sensed but not yet known as Christian. Jesus was embraced in all his humanity and was intimately known as God-with-us.

It is worth noting that during the evangelization of Ireland, there were no martyrs. The pre-Christian culture seems to have prepared the people to readily receive the Christian proclamation. Faith in the Word who became flesh was accepted and embraced. It was natural for these saints to worship the Christ Child in the manger, a baby bearing the full glory of God, cradled among barn animals.

These saints do not split flesh and spirit. We hear, as a deep melody in their lives, a firm and steady faith that spirit and matter go together. The saints lead us to tend the spirit in flesh and the flesh inspirited. They call us to a perception that the divine presence is truly within matter, though never limited to matter. They give us a new orientation, an orientation that leads us to value our embodied lives as cherished by God.

## Bless, O God, the Earth beneath My Feet

The Celtic tradition upholds the Judeo-Christian affirmation that all that is created is inherently and essentially good because all that is created comes from a good and loving God. Because the Creation comes from God, all that is created may be God's means of revelation and testimony. The Creation is sacramental; every bit of the created order points beyond itself to the living Trinity, its source. Thus Saint Patrick sees the very elements of nature as revealing God's mighty power, and Saint Kevin cares for a mother blackbird as one of Christ's creatures. The Celtic church maintained that the faithful have been given two great books of revelation—the Scriptures and the Creation. These two books are to be read in tandem as each informs the other, each illuminates the truth of the other. Reading one without the other can cause misunderstanding and confusion because the Scriptures and the Creation are both from God, given to us for our increasing wisdom and knowledge of God.

The Celtic tradition sees nature and grace as intricately and beautifully interdependent. The goodness of God is known through the essential goodness of nature: the goodness of the landscape we inhabit, the goodness of our very flesh. The human body is known as essentially good, as a means through which one may become aware of God. The senses are seen as God-given means for perceiving, knowing, and acting. Although human behaviors can be sinful, the human body itself is a holy gift, given by the One who has knit us together in our mothers' wombs.

*Companioned by Dear Ones*

The Celtic church, though not free from the negative attitudes toward women that mark Christian history, did, in some instances, model a rich collaboration between men and women. The great women saints, such as Brigit, Ita, and Hilda, often governed what were known as double monasteries. These monastic houses offered formation for both men and women in the same community.

The saints' lives contain many stories of women being sought out for their gifts of spiritual discernment, wisdom, and authority. Saint Brendan, for example, went to Saint Ita for guidance. By the same token, many of the men, such as Saint Cuthbert and Saint Aidan, worked closely with women in spreading the gospel. In the history of the Celtic church, men and women often worked together, living out mutual care and responsibility, spreading the gospel as much through the example of their lives as by their preaching or teaching.

Though there is some debate among scholars about whether women in the Celtic church were admitted to holy orders, it is certainly true that the oral tradition concerning Saint Brigit holds that the prayer of consecration for a bishop was prayed over her. To this day she is often depicted with a crosier (the bishop's staff). Whether or not she actually was a bishop, she continues to be revered as a woman who, as the abbess of the double monastery at Kildare, carried the institutional authority of the church.

*I Yield Me to Thy Cross*

Sin is taken very seriously in the Celtic Christian tradition. Rather than a complete eradication of humanity's essential goodness, sin is conceived as a terrible state of enslavement from which humanity is delivered by the saving action of Jesus Christ. Sin has the effect of deforming the person each one of us is called to be in Christ. Through the redeeming and sanctifying work of the risen Lord, each person is set free from this bondage. Then his or her essential goodness, which had been obscured or entrapped, may be released for the enrichment of the people of God and the building up of the church.

While the essential goodness of creation, the goodness of men and women, was upheld and proclaimed, the Celtic church was very mindful of the destructive power of sin. Many of the stories of these saints include details of rigorous ascetical practice—fasting, praying for long hours in difficult postures, vigils—intended to be offered for the healing of sin. The Celtic church had a strongly ascetical bent, and some of the saints, such as Ita, were chastised by others for being overly zealous in their dedication. Asceticism was balanced by common sense, by a realistic awareness of the need to tend to our bodies as God's gift, and by a suspicion of the "puffing up" (to use Saint Paul's words) that can occur when practices such as fasting are overdone.

*My Walk This Day with Christ*

Jesus is the One who is the companion on the way. The culture of the Celtic lands during the Age of the Saints was strongly rural. The Roman roads never reached Ireland and did not extend deeply into Wales or Scotland. People walked from one place to another, often through difficult terrain. Jesus, friend and companion, was known as the One who accompanied each person on these journeys, blessing, guiding, protecting, befriending. Many of the saints journeyed from place to place, preaching and teaching on the way, patterning their life on the life of Jesus. As they journeyed they prayed to Jesus as the One whose steps matched theirs, the One who granted them succor and guidance when the way became dark and uncertain. The *Carmina Gadelica* contains many prayers for journeys and pilgrimage. The Irish and Welsh traditions also include these journey prayers.

This strong emphasis on Christ accompanying us offers the metaphor of Christ as the One who walks with us throughout our life. He is Emmanuel, God-with-us, whose steps match ours yet also precede and follow ours.

*The Saints Surrounding*

The community of saints is near and familial. To this day there is a tender, homely perception of the saints being close to us and accompanying us in every moment. The Welsh poet Waldo Williams has observed that as current members of a tradition spanning many centuries, Celtic Christians are "keeping house in a cloud of witnesses" (in Thomas, p. 11). The Celtic Christian tradition is keenly aware of the heavenly witnesses who accompany the risen Lord and his people. This particular perspective offers healing to the modern church. The sense that all the faithful who have gone before are present to us through the risen Christ, continuously offering intercession and company, helps us perceive the whole human family as God's family. We begin to be delivered from the profound loneliness that so often characterizes modern life, for we are given a deepening awareness that we are always in the company of this great "cloud of witnesses," whether we are at work, at home, or asleep.

*God in My Life*

The Celtic Christian tradition focuses on the details of everyday living as the locus of faith. All aspects of work and play, life and death have the potential to reveal Christ's presence. These are also sacramental moments that may lead to profound insight, as we discern God's living presence in even the most humble of tasks. Domestic and familial, the prayer tradition offers a vision of daily life lived under "the eye of the great God of glory." The rhythms of living—daily, seasonal, generational—are hallowed through the continual offering of prayer and the habitual remembering of Christ's presence.

Thus every moment of human life may be an occasion for the offering of prayer. From Saint David of Wales, we receive the tradition that it is the "little things" that hold human community together, all those daily tasks that weave us into one fabric. In the Celtic Christian tradition, each person's work is an occasion for offering prayer.

To the Christian of the present day, this practice offers growing awareness that all our actions may be offered to God. Just as Saint David calls us to remember the little things, so we may see that acts like driving in car pools, writing memos, or tracking inventory are all necessary to the careful tending of the web of human relationship.

## The Shape of Christ Be toward You

The Celtic saints lived in times that were uncertain, in times when the Christian faith was a young faith among many other faiths and indigenous traditions. They offer us a glimpse of lives characterized by a gracious confidence in the living God and a down-to-earth awareness of human need. These men and women come to us offering friendship and wisdom and encouraging us every step of the way as we seek to live as faithful Christians. They call us to value the earth as God's creation, to care for one another with reverence and tenderness, to take risks and venture forth with trust in God's guidance. The faith of the Celtic saints is robust, resilient, and lighthearted. They offer us much that is healing and strengthening as we walk with Christ into an unknown future in a new century.

> God's blessing be yours,
> And well may it befall you;
> Christ's blessing be yours,
> And well be you entreated;
> Spirit's blessing be yours,
> And well spend you your lives,
> Each day that you rise up,
> Each night that you lie down.
>
> (*Carmina Gadelica,* p. 257)

# Meditation 1

# Saint Patrick:
# The Encompassing
# Presence of Christ

*Theme:* In Patrick's life, we are given the example of a person who comes to know Christ's presence in every human circumstance.

*Opening prayer:*

> My Christ! my Christ! my shield, my encircler,
> Each day, each night, each light, each dark;
> My Christ! my Christ! my shield, my encircler,
> Each day, each night, each light, each dark.
> Be near me, uphold me, my treasure, my triumph,
> In my lying, in my standing, in my watching, in my
>     sleeping.
> Jesu, Son of Mary! my helper, my encircler,

Jesu, Son of David! my strength everlasting;
Jesu, Son of Mary! my helper, my encircler,
Jesu, Son of David! my strength everlasting.

(*Carmina Gadelica,* pp. 212–13)

## About Patrick

Born about the year 390, Patrick became the patron saint of
Ireland. His life in Christ, however, began rather inauspiciously.
His father was an ordained deacon, and his grandfather was a
priest, but Patrick was not a particularly observant Christian.
He had been baptized, he had learned some prayers, and he
had lived in a Christian household, yet as an adolescent Patrick
felt no real bond to the living faith of the Christian church.
Though he held the faith of his parents at arm's length, he no
doubt absorbed more than he realized.

Then at the age of sixteen, violence interrupted Patrick's
life. Irish slave traders kidnapped the young man. They sold
him as a slave to a petty Irish king, who forced him to work as
a shepherd slave. We know from Patrick's own hand, in the
words of his *Confession,* that this existence was harsh. Gone
were the safety of hearth and home and the stable connections
of kin and friend.

During this time young Patrick began to pray the prayers
that he had learned when he was younger. The words began to
come alive. There in that wild country, with lashing rain and
fearsome wind, Patrick was embraced by the living Christ; he
began to know the prayers as more than words, the belief as
more than doctrine.

One night Patrick heard a voice telling him that a ship was
waiting for him. After six years of praying, waiting, and longing,
Patrick acted on the voice's instruction. He set out on foot, a

runaway slave, relying on the compass of his heart to lead him to the boat promised by God.

Upon his arrival in the south of Ireland, Patrick did indeed find a boat preparing to depart. At first the captain refused his passage, so Patrick went to the hut where he was staying and began to pray. Later a crewman came out and bid Patrick to get on the boat. Patrick's journey home had begun.

Patrick tells us that when he reached home, he received yet another vision, this of a man named Victoricus, who came from Ireland bearing letters. Patrick opened one of the letters and began to read, and as he did, he heard "the voice of the Irish" pleading with him, "We ask thee, boy, come and walk among us once more" (MacDonald, *Saint Patrick,* pp. 35–36). Patrick had escaped slavery and made his way home, only to receive a plea from those who had enslaved him. He was called to be one of God's reconcilers.

He once again left his home, his family, and his friends, but this time he freely chose to depart for Ireland. He made the conscious decision to go to the people who had captured and enslaved him. Having found and been found by Christ in times of deepest fear, estrangement, and trial, Patrick knew Christ would be with him every step of the way; the wisdom he gained in slavery and hardship never left him. His mission to the Irish was unique in history. No blood was shed. No martyrs were slain. He came to his Irish enslavers as friend and reconciler, calling them to recognize the Lord through whom they had been created.

*Pause:* Reflect on a time when you were away from home and family and you experienced Christ's presence.

## Patrick's Words

I saw Him praying in me, and I was as it were within my
body, and I heard Him above me, that is, over the
inward man, and there He prayed mightily with groan-
ings. And all the time I was astonished, and wondered,
and thought with myself who it could be that prayed in
me. But at the end of the prayer He spoke, saying that
He was the Spirit.

(MacDonald, *Saint Patrick,* p. 36)

## Reflection

The tradition of the *lorica,* or breastplate prayer, is closely tied
to Saint Patrick. (*Lorica* is the Latin word used for the breastplate of a Roman soldier's armor.) A *lorica* prayer allows one to
call on the presence of Christ, in whom "all things hold together"
(COLOSSIANS 1:17).

"Saint Patrick's Breastplate" has been translated into
English many times. This excerpt is taken from a version by
Irish scholar Noel Dermott O'Donohue:

For my shield this day I call:
Christ's power in his coming
and in his baptising,
Christ's power in his dying
On the cross, his arising
from the tomb, his ascending;
Christ's power in his coming
for judgment and ending.

(Mackey, p. 47)

- Sit quietly and comfortably. Pray the words of the breast-plate. Imagine the shield of Christ encircling you. What do you feel?

- Take a moment to remember the times when Christ has shielded you. Write them down. Offer thanksgiving for each instance of shielding. Pray for those who need to be shield-ed from harm, from danger, from violence.

- Another verse of Patrick's breastplate leads us to claim Christ's all-pervading presence:

> Christ beside me, Christ before me;
> Christ behind me, Christ within me;
> Christ beneath me, Christ above me;
> Christ to right of me, Christ to left of me;
> Christ in my lying, my sitting, my rising;
> Christ in heart of all who know me,
> Christ on tongue of all who meet me,
> Christ in eye of all who see me,
> Christ in ear of all who hear me.
>
> (Mackey, p. 48)

Pray this prayer as you take a walk, as you go about your daily work, as you drive. (You may want to write it on a small card.) This is a prayer that is very portable; it is to be prayed while we are on the way. Allow the prayer to accompany you wherever you go.

At the end of the day, make note of when and where the prayer helped you to perceive Christ's presence in your activities, in those whom you encountered, in a challenging situation. Practice this way of praying for several days.

What changes do you notice in your perception? How do
you feel about those changes?

## God's Word

*Likewise the Spirit helps us in our weakness; for we do not know
how to pray as we ought, but that very Spirit intercedes with sighs
too deep for words. And God, who searches the heart, knows what
is the mind of the Spirit, because the Spirit intercedes for the
saints according to the will of God.*

(ROMANS 8:26–27)

*Closing prayer:* Gracious Lord Jesus Christ, I am thanking you
in my lying down and in my rising up, in my waking and in my
sleeping, in my speaking and in my working. May my life and
the lives of all I meet be filled with your radiant presence.
Amen.

## Meditation 2

# Saint Brigit:
# Soul Friendship

*Theme:* Brigit, by her compassion and spiritual wisdom, embodies the Celtic tradition of soul friendship. Her concern for those in need and the generosity of her listening heart remind us that God is very near when we are in the company of a true soul friend. Such relationships transcend both time and place.

*Opening prayer:*

> Every day and every night
> That I say the genealogy of Bride,
> I shall not be killed, I shall not be harried,
> I shall not be put in cell, I shall not be wounded,
> Neither shall Christ leave me in forgetfulness.
>
> (Carmina Gadelica, p. 81)

## About Brigit

From the beginning of her life, Brigit, also known as Bride or
Brigid and as Ffraid in Wales, was touched by God. She was
born of a king and a slave around the year 452, and is said to
have been raised by a teacher who saw in her a radiant daughter who would shine like the sun among the stars of heaven.
From an early age, Brigit showed compassion for the poor and
a generous responsiveness to those in need. The fire of the
Holy Spirit appeared to accompany her wherever she traveled;
numerous stories tell of a flame of fire that others would see
about her head. When Brigit went forward to receive the veil of
religious life, the fire of the Holy Spirit seemed to be with her.
As she knelt to receive the veil, the bishop said the words of
ordination for a bishop, and when his assistant protested that
such a prayer should not be said over a woman, the bishop
replied: "No power have I in this matter. That dignity has been
given by God unto Brigid, beyond every other woman"
(MacDonald, *Saint Bride,* p. 27).

Brigit took this blessing and founded the great monastery
at Kildare. (*Kildare* means "church of the oak" in old Irish.) Here
both men and women received her guidance and leadership as
abbess and soul friend. She was recognized in all of Ireland as
one aflame with the intensity of Christ's love for the poor. Her
spiritual discernment was manifest in seeing even the smallest
needs of another's body and soul. Many stories recount how
she healed the wretched, the foolish, and the weak. From the
oral tradition we learn that Brigit declared, "It is in the name of
Christ I feed the poor, for Christ is in the body of every poor
person." She practiced a ministry of Christian hospitality, welcoming one and all in the name of Christ.

Because she was fostered by another family and nurtured

as a Christian, Brigit had a distinctly Irish perspective on friendship. She honored and lived out the tradition of having an *anam cara,* or soul friend. Her life was typified by a profound sense of Christ's friendship with us, a sense that is foundational to Christian soul friendship.

From Celtic tradition we receive the story that one of Brigit's own foster sons came to spend time with her at Kildare. While he was there, Brigit knew in prayer that her foster son's soul friend had suddenly died. She counseled him and advised him to find a new soul friend quickly.

In the Irish tradition, the earthly soul friend was always accompanied by heavenly soul friends. Those holy souls who had entered the gates of eternity were perceived to be alive in Christ and readily accessible to those on earth. In prayer, one could ask that the saintly presences, whose lives had been icons of the life of the risen Lord, be our protectors, guides, and intercessors. Because the soul friends of the community of saints were always present to the faithful, Christians were perceived as being never alone, no matter what the circumstances.

One of the most significant traditions about Brigit depicts her as the midwife and nursemaid at the birth of Jesus. To the Irish, Brigit abides in eternity; this seemingly fanciful belief reveals a perception that Brigit's way of caring and ministering were learned at the manger, amid the oxen and the cattle. She is seen as the companion of the Holy Family, as Mary's trusted friend and aid-woman, and as the kind and faithful nurse to the Christ Child.

There is truth in the story, for Brigit lived her life encountering the human family as the Holy Family, and her sisters at Kildare as fellow nursemaids of Jesus. This tradition of Brigit as the nursemaid of Christ continues to this day in Ireland, Scotland, and Wales, and reminds us that the Holy Family is always in our midst.

*Pause:* Reflect on what a soul friend means to you.

## Brigit's Words

"Anyone without a soul friend is like a body without a
head." (Sellner, p. 73)

## Reflection

The tradition of *anam cara,* or soul friendship, is closely tied to
the Celtic saints, especially Saint Brigit. She was known to have
guided both men and women in their spiritual journey. A wise
soul friend such as Brigit served as a mentor and a guide, but
most of all as a companion along the way. One recognizes a
soul friend by the hospitality she or he offers in accepting one's
deepest thoughts and aspirations. With a soul friend, one feels
at home not only in this world but also in the greater world of
spirit. The soul friend honors the secrets of the heart and
gently nudges one's dreams into being.

It is in soul friendship that one discovers the presence of
Christ. When Jesus says that whenever two or three are gathered in his name, he will be with them, we see the true meaning of soul friendship.

Soul friendship can extend beyond geographic time and
space. A soul friend may be someone we encounter in our reading or in our prayer. Brigit herself continues to minister to
those who seek her companionship and guidance. She is especially a soul friend to those who seek to make holy the ordinary
tasks of daily life.

- Spend some time remembering the soul friends who have
  appeared in your life. What gifts have they given you? Take

some time and write those friends a note expressing gratitude for their gifts.

- Remember a time when you felt without a soul friend. What
  was happening at this time of your life? Where did you go for
  companionship? What lessons did you learn about yourself?

- Sometimes we are called to be a soul friend to someone
  seeking guidance. Who do you feel is calling you to be a
  soul friend? Which of the following qualities do you feel you
  could offer? In which area do you desire more growth?
  - compassion
  - truthfulness
  - humility
  - prayerfulness
  - wisdom
  - generosity

- In the Celtic understanding of time, one lives in both the
  present and in eternity. Saint Brigit, in her vocation of
  showing mercy in the love of Christ, was often pictured as
  the nursemaid of Jesus, present in spirit to help both Mary
  and Jesus in their times of need.
  - Imagine yourself being present at the birth of Christ.
  - Imagine Mary and Joseph as they attend to the
    Christ Child.
  - Picture the shepherds and any other visitors as they
    enter the stable.
  - Watch the donkey and the sheep as they sleep
    peacefully.
  - Where are you in this scene? What is your relation-
    ship to the Christ Child?

- Saint Brigit has often been considered a soul friend by those who tend to the domestic tasks of living. Many of the prayers collected in the *Carmina Gadelica* demonstrate the blessing of being among Brigit's companions.

> I am under the shielding
> Of good Brigit each day;
> I am under the shielding
> Of good Brigit each night.
> I am under the keeping
> Of the Nurse of Mary,
> Each early and late,
> Every dark, every light.
> Brigit is my comrade-woman,
> Brigit is my maker of song,
> Brigit is my helping-woman,
> My choicest of women, my guide.
>
> (*Carmina Gadelica*, p. 239)

What soul friend accompanies you each day and each night, in your work and in your leisure? Write a prayer about such a friend in the style of the Celtic prayer above.

## God's Word

*You are my friends if you do what I command you. I do not call you servants any longer, because the servant does not know what the master is doing; but I have called you friends, because I have made known to you everything that I have heard from my Father.*
(JOHN 15:14–15)

*Closing prayer:* I give you thanks, most gracious God, for calling me into friendship with you and for giving me soul friends as companions along the way. Grant me the wisdom, grace, and mercy to be a soul friend to others, for your mercy's sake. Amen.

# Meditation 3

# Saint Non of Wales: Holy Mothering

*Theme:* Saint Non of Wales was dedicated to holy mothering and to the continuing birth of new communities and new life in maturity. Her presence with us in prayer also helps us to discern when it is time to let go of those we have mothered and begin a new phase of our life.

*Opening prayer:*

> There is a mother's heart in the heart of God.
>
> (Reith, p. 5)

## About Non

Much beloved by the people of Wales, Saint Non was the mother of Saint David, the patron saint of that country. Because of her caring and nurturing ways with David, Non is seen as a holy mother. Her strong mothering of David led to a strong church in Wales, and she is regarded as the holy mother of the Welsh church.

Non's story begins with the violent disruption of her life. Beautiful, of royal lineage, a maiden of Christian devotion and faithfulness, Non drew the attention of Sanctus, a king of the region in which she lived. Sanctus was seized by lust at the sight of Non. He overpowered her, dishonored her, and raped her. In this act of violence, David was conceived. According to the traditional accounts, the earth itself responded to David's conception: two standing stones came forth from the earth, one at Non's head and one at her feet. Creation itself recognized that a saintly child would come forth from Non's womb.

During her pregnancy, with new life swelling within her, Non continued to live a holy life dedicated to the living God. In the ascetic tradition of the Celtic saints, she lived on bread and water, prayed, and trusted that the child within her, though savagely conceived, would be a gift for her people. One day, hungry for a word of the gospel, she went to hear a preacher in a local church. As she entered the sanctuary, the preacher found himself unable to speak. He dismissed the congregation and tried to discern what caused his sudden inability to preach. Non, in the meantime, hid in the church, hoping to feed on the living Word should the preacher begin again. He tried once more to preach, but could do no more than speak conversationally. In fear and frustration, he bid that if anyone were hiding in the sanctuary, she or he should come forth. Non said, "I am hiding here," and emerged from hiding. He asked her to depart, and she did. The congregation entered the church once more, and the preacher was able to preach. It was evident that the child she was bearing was of God, and that the child's presence was more powerful than the preacher's voice.

When the time came for David to be born, Non was walking along the cliffs above the sea. As her labor began, a fierce storm broke out. Lightning, thunder, and great waves accompanied the rhythmic contractions of her womb. Hail and rain poured down. Yet at the place where Non labored, a brilliant light shone and no rain fell. Non gripped a standing stone as the contractions grew stronger, leaving on the stone a print of her hands. It is said that the stone broke in half, the very elements having compassion for Non as she brought forth David in the wild solitude of the cliffs above the sea. Once the baby was born, a spring came forth from the ground, pure water for baptism erupting from the creation, responding to the mother's faithfulness and courage. Thus the stones of the old religion bore the very mark of Non's hands, the mark of a follower of Christ bringing forth new life despite her own violation.

After David was born, he was sent to live with a foster family in a neighboring region, as was the custom with children from prominent families in Britain and Ireland. He was fostered by the family of a bishop, while Non went to Cornwall at the request of her sister and founded a church at Altarnon. The church was complemented by a holy well known for its healing properties.

After a time in Cornwall, Non ventured to Brittany. She is said to have lived a holy life there; her example brought others to the way of Christ. Many place names in this part of France bear her name.

*Pause:* When in your life have you been mothered by someone other than your mother?

## Non's Words

"I am hiding here."

(Sellner, p. 177)

## Reflection

Non's life directs us to attend to the call to mother one another, whether we are men or women. This is often a hidden vocation, lived out in the most ordinary aspects of human relationship. Non experienced violation and degradation, but she brought forth a holy child from that experience. She demonstrated faithful mothering as she labored to bring David forth, as she sought proper fostering for him, and as she moved into her own proper vocation and ministry after his birth. Non calls us to ask ourselves to whom we are called to mother. She calls us to be aware of those who may need nurturing, protection, or shelter in the storm of life. She leads us to see that mothering is a hard, physical, risky task, yet a task that is essential to the continual renewing and building up of the people of God.

Non also guides us in the gentle art of letting go, of allowing our children, whether biological or spiritual, to step into their own lives and vocations as we further explore our own. Her life continued to deepen in faith and fruitfulness after she had borne David. Her ministry did not end when he came of age for fostering; her ministry acquired new depth and richness as she, a single woman, traveled to Cornwall and Brittany, spreading the gospel.

- What hidden, sacred life in you is waiting to be mothered? Sit still. Take the time to center, to tend to the breath of life that flows in and out of your lungs. Place your hands palms up in your lap. Imagine that you are holding the hidden, sacred life that the living Christ wishes to bring forth in you. What images arise? What colors or shapes do you see? What yearnings do you begin to feel? Make note of these in your journal. Return to this exercise from time to time for a growing sense of what you need to mother within you.

- Who have been your mothering influences? These could be men or women, mentors, leaders, friends, or family. Write their names down, along with a description of the qualities of mothering with which each has gifted you. Thank God for each of these persons. If it is appropriate and possible, write to them thanking them for their care and nurturing.

- We often bear the "handprints" of those who have mothered us, just as the standing stone bore the handprints of Non. Whose handprints do you bear? How have those imprints formed you? Take a piece of paper and trace your own hand. Give thanks for your hands, for your handiwork. In the Celtic Christian prayer tradition, one often asks for a blessing of "the handling of my hand." Write a prayer asking this blessing and inscribe it on the paper with your handprint.

- One way to mother our children is to bless them. Write a prayer of blessing for your children, whether they are yours by birth or by spirit.

## God's Word

> O Lord, I am not proud;*
> I have no haughty looks.
> I do not occupy myself with great matters,*
> or with things that are too hard for me.
> But I still my soul and make it quiet,
> like a child upon its mother's breast;*
> my soul is quieted within me.
> O Israel, wait upon the Lord,*
> from this time forth for evermore.

(PSALM 131)

*Closing prayer:* Living God, you have knit me together in my mother's womb, and you call me to the holy mothering of others for the sake of your Son, Jesus Christ. Grant me the eyes to see those I am called to care for and nurture, that I may help in the birthing of your new creation, by the power of your Holy Spirit. Amen.

# Meditation 4

# Saint David of Wales: Community

*Theme:* Saint David, the patron saint of Wales, calls us to be mindful of the small, hidden acts that weave together human community. His life and his counsel lead us to tend our neighbors' needs out of deep gratitude for all that we have been given.

*Opening prayer:*

> God to enfold me,
> God to surround me,
> God in my speaking,
> God in my thinking.
> God in my sleeping,
> God in my waking,
> God in my watching,
> God in my hoping.
> God in my life,
> God in my lips,

God in my hands,
God in my heart.
God in my sufficing,
God in my slumber,
God in mine ever-living soul,
God in mine eternity.

                                    (*Carmina Gadelica,* pp. 204–5)

## About David

The story of Saint David begins with his auspicious birth in the early sixth century. He was born to Saint Non in the midst of a strong thunderstorm, on the rocky cliffs above the bay. Though rain, lightning, and thunder filled the air, the sacred place of David's birth was filled with light and serenity.

As a young boy, David, also known as Dewi in Welsh, was sent to the family of a bishop to be fostered. In the custom of the Celtic peoples, children from prominent families in a region were often raised by foster families in neighboring regions. This custom formed networks and created interdependent social ties that strengthened the community and gave the child the advantage of having a large extended family.

From an early age, David was dedicated to the church. Consequently his education prepared him for a life of Christian service. He studied in tutorial fashion, learning the Scriptures, history, and tradition.

Some twelve monasteries are said to have been founded by David. He established his last monastic settlement at the site of the present-day town of Saint David's in southwest Wales on the Pembrokeshire coast. In time David became both abbot and bishop; his leadership was recognized and welcomed. He is also said to have been a worker of miracles—his first miracle was to restore the sight of his teacher Paulinus.

David is said to have been around six feet tall and very strong. He never shirked physical labor. Though he lived mainly on water, vegetables, and herbs, he was capable of pulling a plough like an ox. He chose to live a simple life, dedicated to Christ. Despite his personal austerity, David was noted for treating others with respect and kindness. His words and his way of life encouraged many to join his community, and it is his emphasis on community, rather than his asceticism, that continues to influence Christianity in Wales.

In the monasteries that David founded, all was owned in common. The word *my* was not used. Each monk entered the monastery literally naked, a gesture symbolic of human dependence on God's mercy and providence.

By all accounts David was a man of true kindness, dedicated to a life of service in the name of his Lord. Humane interaction characterized his dealings with all people—old and young, rich and poor, stranger and friend. At his death his community gathered in sorrow. As David lay dying, he reminded the people gathered that they were to follow his example, to care for one another in "the little things," and those dying words have had a lasting impact on the Christians of Wales. As scholar Patrick Thomas points out in a discussion of David's influence, "In any community apparently insignificant acts of habitual kindness and self-forgetfulness which display a fundamental respect and love for others can generate stability, unity and wholeness" (p. 128).

*Pause:* When has another's care of the little things made you aware of Christ's care and mercy for you?

## David's Words

> Lords, brothers and sisters, be happy and keep your
> faith and your belief, and do the little things that you
> have heard and seen me do.
>
> (Thomas, p. 127)

## Reflection

David's life calls us to tend to the little things. As our companion in prayer, he helps us to have eyes to see and ears to hear the daily, ordinary tasks that we might accomplish for the good of our respective communities. We are led to a quality of attention in our prayer, a quality that allows us to remember the ways we are continuously cared for and the ways we are called to offer care. David's life gives us an example of living mindfully. He calls us to seek gentle and constant awareness of the needs of others so that we might act in little ways that build up community in Christ. David's way also calls us to offer these little acts in joy, bringing delight to our neighbors.

- Make a list of five people whose tending of the little things has helped to deepen your life as a Christian. Thank God for the life of each one.

- Offer a hidden act of support for another (a prayer, an anonymous card or gift). You could choose a person who is struggling with a problem, someone who is ill, a person who is lonely, a friend who is having a hard time. There are any number of possibilities. Seek to be creative and kind in your offering.

- One of the more cynical perspectives in our society holds that the action of one person cannot change anything. Pick a charity or a social agency whose ministry you support. Send a contribution, become a dues-paying member, or support the endeavors of the larger organization.

- In the Celtic Christian prayer tradition, attention is given to each aspect of our daily interaction as a potential encounter with the living God. Pray the following prayer slowly, remembering with each line ways that the petition might be enfleshed in your life. Add movement and gesture if you wish.

> Bless to me, O God,
> My soul and my body;
> Bless to me, O God,
> My belief and my condition;
> Bless to me, O God,
> My heart and my speech,
> And bless to me, O God,
> The handling of my hand;
> Strength and busyness of morning,
> Habit and temper of modesty,
> Force and wisdom of thought,
> And Thine own path, O God of virtues,
> Till I go to sleep this night;
> Thine own path, O God of virtues,
> Till I go to sleep this night.

(*Carmina Gadelica*, p. 197)

## God's Word

*Then the king will say to those at his right hand, "Come, you that are blessed by my Father, inherit the kingdom prepared for you from the foundation of the world; for I was hungry and you gave me food, I was thirsty and you gave me something to drink, I was a stranger and you welcomed me, I was naked and you gave me clothing, I was sick and you took care of me, I was in prison and you visited me." Then the righteous will answer him, "Lord, when was it that we saw you hungry and gave you food, or thirsty and gave you something to drink? And when was it that we saw you a stranger and welcomed you, or naked and gave you clothing? And when was it that we saw you sick or in prison and visited you?" And the king will answer them, "Truly I tell you, just as you did it to one of the least of these who are members of my family, you did it to me."*

(MATTHEW 25:34–40)

*Closing prayer:* Holy and living Trinity, grant me the grace and wisdom to see the little things you would have me do, and the humility and charity to do them. Amen.

# Meditation 5

# Saint Columba: Christian Vision

*Theme:* Saint Columba, who is lovingly named the Dove of the Church, inspires us with a Christian vision that infuses the creativity of our human gifts with the gifts of the Holy Spirit. He calls us to devote ourselves entirely to a vision of Christ that has the power to transform the world.

*Opening prayer:*

> Be thou my vision, O Lord of my heart,
> Naught be all else to me, save that thou art.
> Thou my best thought by day or by night,
> Waking or sleeping, Thy presence my light.
>
> (An ancient Irish hymn)

## About Columba

Columba's life began with a vision. His mother, who was born
of royal lineage in the northern part of Ireland, was expecting a
princely son who would be a king. Before his birth, however,
she received a dream in which the angels told her that her son
would be a great prophet destined to be the leader of innumer-
able souls. Heeding the angel's message, she sent the young
Columba to the great teachers of the Christian faith. His excep-
tional gifts in poetry and expression were nurtured in the tradition of the great bards of Ireland. From the very beginning he
showed a love of the psalms.

Columba's prayers revealed to people that he possessed
what the Celts call the gift of "second sight," a quickened inner
vision that allows one to transcend time and space, to see eternity in the midst of the everyday details of life.

This inner vision led Columba to found monastic communities all over Ireland. It is said that he founded forty-one
monasteries in forty-one years, many of these monasteries
becoming centers of prayer, hospitality, and learning.

However, Columba's love of learning caused a conflict in the
monastery at Moville. He was accused of copying a book of psalms
that belonged to another monk. The case went to the High King
of Ireland, who ruled that Columba had to return the copy to the
owner of the original text. What began as a dispute over property,
a copied book of psalms, erupted into armed battle. Columba's
supporters fought and won, supposedly demonstrating his
power. Columba, and Ireland, saw the destruction that posses-
siveness and greed had caused; more than three thousand soldiers
died in the battle. In an effort to make amends for this misuse of
power, Columba's beloved Ireland forced him into exile. He then
embarked on a pilgrimage, entrusting himself to God's mercy.

He set sail in 563 with twelve companions. They landed on the ancient isle of Iona on the northwest coast of present-day Scotland. Landing on the day of the feast of Pentecost, Columba found his vision of Christ's mercy and forgiveness renewed. He began creating one of the greatest centers of faith and evangelism in Christian history. At a time when all was in disarray on the continent of Europe, Iona was a community devoted to learning and to intentional Christian living. Columba's group of monastics sent forth missionaries to evangelize the Picts and the Scots in what is now northern Scotland. Later missionaries from Iona went to Europe and established new monastic foundations, taking the light of the gospel to the farthest reaches of Europe, even as far as Russia.

At the heart of this great flowering of the gospel, Columba maintained a simple, devoted life sustained by his rule of prayer, silence, work, and study. It was said that his face began to reflect the joy of the Spirit, and that even when he was not present, his spirit offered healing and comfort to his fellow monks. His vision of the Christian life continues to thrive today on the island of Iona, where countless pilgrims are inspired by this gifted saint's vision.

*Pause:* Reflect on your own vision of Christ and how that vision takes form in your life.

## Columba's Words

> Let me bless almighty God, whose power extends over sea and land, whose angels watch over all.
> Let me study sacred books to calm my soul; I pray for peace, kneeling at heaven's gates.
> Let me do my daily work, gathering seaweed, catching

fish, giving food to the poor.
Let me say my daily prayers, sometimes chanting,
sometimes quiet, always thanking God.
Delightful it is to live on a peaceful isle, in a quiet cell,
serving the King of kings.

(Van de Weyer, p. 64)

## Reflection

Columba's vision was formed by his passionate love of the truth of the Scriptures and the beauty of creation. As a young monk, he enthusiastically offered his abundant gifts of scholarship, leadership, and poetry in following that vision. At the time of his exile, his vision was shaped by his own experience of sin and failure, exile, redemption, and renewal. From the ashes of Columba's life in Ireland, the living Christ kindled a new life in the saint and gave him the strength to create a new community.

Columba reveals to us a Christian vision that transcends time and space, yet is grounded in our own time. This vision reaches far beyond our grasp, yet it is within our reach. It honors our unique human gifts and multiplies them in service to the world. To pray with Columba is to catch a glimpse of that vision and to join him in devotion, serving the King of kings.

- Although Columba had an inspired vision of God's will, his own personal vision sometimes conflicted with that inspired vision. Reflect for a moment: Have you ever held on to your own vision until it began to thwart God's holy vision? Express your sorrows over any hurt or loss you might have inflicted on others. Spend some time praying that even this loss, like Columba's, will be transformed and made new by God's grace.

- No one receives a vision for oneself alone. A Christian vision is always manifest in the building of community. Columba's vision was manifest in a devout rule of life, in artistic creations such as the illuminated gospels of the Book of Kells, and in the training of missionaries. Today at the Iona Community, which was founded by the Presbyterian minister George MacLeod in 1938, Columba's Christian vision inspires and encourages Christians of many different traditions.

  How is your vision of Christ being made manifest in your life? Focus on these four areas:
  - acting compassionately toward others
  - expressing creativity
  - speaking out for justice and forgiveness
  - inspiring and leading others

- Columba's prayer life was rooted in specific places. His greatest longing was for Derry in Ireland, the place of the oak trees. He seemed to have the Celtic understanding of the "thin places," those places where heaven and earth are closely connected, where the divine presence is acutely felt.

  Close your eyes and return to a special place where you have felt the nearness of God. What do you see? Is it a solitary place? Are others around you? Listen quietly. What sounds do you hear? Is there anything you might want to touch or hold in your hand? What does this place say to you about God? About yourself? If the place is nearby, make a pilgrimage there as often as you can.

- The Scriptures were an important part of Celtic prayer. The psalms were especially loved by the monks, including Columba. As he was preparing to die, Columba's last act of devotion was to copy Psalm 34. When he came to the verse that reads "Fear the Lord, you that are his saints, for those who fear him lack nothing," he stopped and went out to bless the monastery.

What is your favorite psalm? Take a clean sheet of paper and copy the words slowly and reverently, allowing the act of copying to express your devotion to God. If you are so inclined, adorn your manuscript with color and design.

## God's Word

> Then afterward
> I will pour out my spirit on all flesh;
> your sons and your daughters shall
> prophesy, your old men shall dream dreams,
> and your young men shall see
> visions.
>
> (Joel 2:28)

*Closing prayer:* Gracious God, cleanse my sight that I may behold you in all things, perceiving your glory in your creation, your people, your Word. Grant me the grace and the courage to live a life shaped by holy vision, that others may come to know and love you. Amen.

# Meditation 6

# Saint Melangell of Wales: A Place of Refuge

*Theme:* Saint Melangell reminds us that in prayer we find a place of refuge where God's protective mantle surrounds us with love.

*Opening prayer:*

> I am placing my soul and my body
> On Thy sanctuary this night, O God,
> On Thy sanctuary, O Jesus Christ,
> On Thy sanctuary, O Spirit of perfect truth;
> The Three who would defend my cause,
> Nor turn Their backs upon me.
> Thou, Father, who art kind and just,
> Thou, Son, who didst overcome death,
> Thou, Holy Spirit of power,
> Be keeping me this night from harm;
> The Three who would justify me
> Keeping me this night and always.
>
> (Carmina Gadelica, p. 54)

## About Melangell

Our knowledge of the life of Saint Melangell comes to us from a seventeenth-century manuscript, but her spirit has permeated the valley of the Bergwyns in Wales since the seventh century. The story of her life begins in Ireland, where she was said to be the daughter of an Irish chieftain. At an early age, she felt an authentic call to a life of prayer and solitude. However, this vocation did not appeal to her parents. Forced to choose between her heart's desire and her parents' wishes, she ran away in search of a place to practice her prayer. She found a safe and welcoming haven in a beautiful, secluded valley in the little kingdom of Powys in the center of Wales.

Melangell's story is shaped by an encounter she had with a local prince in the year 604. The prince was hunting on horseback with his dogs in a place called Pennant when suddenly his dogs went after a fleeing hare. The hare escaped to a thicket of brambles where he found Melangell silently praying. Sensing in her presence a place of refuge, the hare hid under the hem of her garment. When the prince approached the thicket, he ordered his dogs to race forward, but they withdrew in the presence of the saint's strength and holiness. The prince was humbled, and he sought to learn the mystery of Melangell's life. She told him her story of coming to the valley and explained her dedication to a life of prayer. He honored her vocation by declaring that from that time forward, the valley would become a sanctuary for men, women, and animals who came to seek refuge and protection.

Melangell accepted the prince's gift and gathered a community of women to join her. The valley indeed became known as a holy place of prayer where anyone in danger or distress could find a safe haven, and as a sanctuary for wild animals. Melangell is often depicted with hares joining her in her prayers.

In the years after Melangell's death, the place came to be known as Pennant Melangell and was a site of pilgrimage for those seeking healing or hoping to escape oppression. Today the little church that was built in the valley continues the tradition of prayer and refuge for wandering souls, a tradition begun through Melangell's pure desire for prayer and solitude.

*Pause:* Is prayer a place of refuge for you?

## Melangell's Words

I fled from my native soil and under the guidance of God came here in order that I might serve God . . . with my heart and pure body until my dying days.

> (Allchin, *Pennant Melangell*, p. 44)

The continuation of this, Melangell's first testimony of prayer, is reflected in the words inscribed on the lych-gate of the entrance to the present-day shrine at Pennant Melangell: "Turn purely to prayer. Keep your heart for worship. To God the only goodness here give fitting honour."

## Reflection

From the beginning of Melangell's story, we witness her flight to a place that only God could provide. In prayer we experience the full assurance that God is our refuge. Often in the midst of despair or in an experience of being surrounded by enemies, we find that prayer is the place where we are sure to be safe and protected by God's loving care.

To pray with Melangell is to stop our frantic efforts to escape the situations that cause fear and anxiety within us and

to draw near to Christ, who longs to gather us like a mother
hen gathers her young beneath her wings.

In the sanctuary of prayer is the freedom to roam and to be
at peace no matter what external conflicts might be evident. A
person who has experienced the refuge of God in prayer
becomes a place of refuge for others.

- When have you experienced another person as a place of
  refuge? Remember that time. What feelings did you have?
  How was your life changed by experiencing this person as
  a refuge?

- The image of the hare seeking refuge under the skirts of
  Melangell evokes a feminine image of God as one who
  would gather her loved ones under the shadow of her
  wings. Imagine yourself resting peacefully and safely under
  God's wing. What does this feel like? Note the ways your
  body responds. What do you notice? What color are the
  feathers of the wings? How do they feel? If you desire, gather
  fallen feathers in the days ahead as a reminder of God's
  wings covering you.

- The valley where Melangell lived and prayed is a sacred
  place that evokes a sense of peace and sanctuary. The
  counsel to "turn purely to prayer" seems to envelop those
  who enter this space. Find a place in your own home that
  provides a sanctuary for you. It can be a special rocking
  chair, a place by a window, or a home altar with a sacred
  object of faith. Pray at this place often, and learn to receive
  the grace that your prayers can bring.

- A Welsh poet, Ruth Bidgood, has identified with the hare in

Melangell's story. Her poem "Hare at Pennant" expresses the hare's fears:

> I huddle at your feet
> In your garment's folds
> And am simple hare, fool hare, hunted hare.
> I have doubled and doubled,
> Am spent, blown, not a trick left
> To baffle pursuers.
> A leap of despair
> Has brought me to you.
>
> (Allchin, *Pennant Melangell,* p. 34)

Reflect for a moment on your greatest fears. How are you like the hare, trying to run from what haunts you? Express in the form of a prayer whatever fear may bring you to the shelter of God's garment.

• As Melangell's prayer provided a spirit of refuge, so did the place where she prayed. Today we have places of refuge for people needing shelter from violence, oppression, and abuse. These places incarnate the protective love of God. Is God calling you to participate in one of these places through prayer, support, or action? If so, what small step do you need to take to begin participating?

## God's Word

> He who dwells in the shelter of the Most High,*
> abides under the shadow of the Almighty.
> He shall say to the Lord,
> "You are my refuge and my stronghold,*

my God in whom I put my trust."
He shall deliver you from the snare of the hunter*
and from the deadly pestilence.
He shall cover you with his pinions,
and you shall find refuge under his wings.*

(PSALM 91:1–4a)

*Closing prayer:* Gracious God, you enfold us in the soft wings of your love. Grant us refuge in you when we are weary and in need of shelter. Amen.

## Meditation 7

# Saint Ninian of Whithorn: Pioneer in the Faith

*Theme:* Saint Ninian was one of the pioneers of the Christian faith. He established a center for prayer and learning in a remote region of western Scotland in the late fourth century, thereby bringing Christian life and practice into the midst of his culture. Praying with Ninian leads us to be pioneers in the faith.

*Opening prayer:*

> Bless to me, O God,
> Each thing mine eye sees;
> Bless to me, O God,
> Each sound mine ear hears;
> Bless to me, O God,
> Each odour that goes to my nostrils;
> Bless to me, O God,
> Each taste that goes to my lips;
> Each note that goes to my song,

Each ray that guides my way,
Each thing that I pursue,
Each lure that tempts my will,
The zeal that seeks my living soul,
The Three that seek my heart,
The zeal that seeks my living soul,
The Three that seek my heart.

(Carmina Gadelica, p. 199)

## About Ninian

Ninian was born about 360 C.E. in the area of Scotland that is
known today as Dumfries and Galloway. His father was a priest,
and his family practiced the Christian faith, but their society
was a mix of different faiths. In kindness and care, Ninian
brought the gospel to new cultures and peoples. The short catechism traditionally attributed to Ninian gives a hint of the
wellspring of inspiration that characterized his ministry—
Ninian perceived Christ's presence in the world and set forth
expecting to meet him.

We know little about his life before the building of his foundation at Whithorn in modern-day southwestern Scotland,
though it appears that he journeyed to Rome. There he was
formed as a priest and a bishop. On his way back home, he
spent time at Saint Martin of Tours's community in Gaul (modern France). This visit gave Ninian the idea of forming such a
community in his own land. Upon receiving this inspiration, he
returned to his own people, ready to create in their midst a center of Christian prayer and learning.

Ninian founded a site that became known as Candida Casa,
or Whithorn in his native language, meaning "white house." He
brought artisans from Saint Martin's community with him, and

they helped construct a church on top of a plain, close to the coast. From this center Ninian and others went out to speak the Good News to the Picts, who inhabited southern Scotland. We do not know precisely how far Ninian's travels took him, but we do know that he must have had some success converting the chieftains; through their conversions the tribes began to live as Christians.

We know Ninian's life because of the fruit it bore. Though we do not know much of him personally, what we do know is telling. He had the courage and the desire to travel the long distance to Rome to seek formation. In a time when the power and the order of the Roman Empire were under increasing assault, he founded his monastic center at Whithorn, thereby beginning a concerted effort to bring the Christian faith to his homeland. The fruit of Ninian's life continues to become more apparent as archaeological finds reveal more about his mission.

During the Middle Ages, Whithorn became a site of pilgrimage. In recent years the pilgrimage to Whithorn has been taken up again. Year after year people travel to Whithorn to pray and to seek inspiration.

*Pause:* Who are the pioneers of the Christian faith who have influenced you?

## Ninian's Words

*Ninian's Catechism*

> QUESTION: What is best in the world?
> ANSWER: To do the will of our Maker.
> QUESTION: What is his will?
> ANSWER: That we should live according to the laws of his creation.

QUESTION: How do we know those laws?
ANSWER: By study—studying the Scriptures with devotion.
QUESTION: What tool has our Maker provided for this study?
ANSWER: The intellect, which can probe everything.
QUESTION: And what is the fruit of study?
ANSWER: To perceive the eternal Word of God reflected in every plant and insect, every bird and animal, and every man and woman.

(Van de Weyer, pp. 177–78)

## Reflection

Ninian was a pioneer of the faith. His life bore much fruit. He established Whithorn, went on missions to the Picts of southern Scotland, and established churches. We know of his life because of the fruit his faith bore. Though he lived in the late fourth century, his legacy lives on, calling us to remember that what we do during our time on earth can have singular and lasting effects.

- Whose life and witness has made a difference in your life? Give thanks for those persons. What fruit do you see developing in your own journey of faith? How do you hope to be remembered?

- Ninian's catechism reveals a profound sense of the indwelling spirit of the living Christ to be encountered in "every plant and insect, every bird and animal, and every man and woman" (Van de Weyer, p. 178). The incarnate Christ permeates all creation. How have you encountered the living Christ in nature? Write down what was revealed to you. What were your feelings? How was your faith deepened?

- How have you encountered the living Christ in another person? Have you ever been surprised by Christ's presence in another person? Make note of those encounters. What do you discern about Christ's presence in your life through those moments? How were you changed? What did you learn about yourself through those meetings?

- Near Whithorn is a place called Ninian's Cave. Tradition associates the saint with this hollowed-out place above the sea; it is said that he went to this cave to pray and to seek the presence of the living God. Today many people make pilgrimages to this site, seeking a sense of the holy. What places in your life have been special places of prayer? Where do you pray now? Which places impart a sense of the holy to you? Give thanks for the presence of the living God in those places, and ask for increasing awareness of God's presence in each plant and insect, each bird and animal, each place and time.

## God's Word

*Therefore, since we are surrounded by so great a cloud of witnesses, let us also lay aside every weight and the sin that clings so closely, and let us run with perseverance the race that is set before us, looking to Jesus the pioneer and perfecter of our faith, who for the sake of the joy that was set before him endured the cross, disregarding its shame, and has taken his seat at the right hand of the throne of God.*

(HEBREWS 12:1–2)

*Closing prayer:* God grant me the courage to grow in faith, the gift of joy that births that courage, and the love of Christ that creates the joy, that I may be a pioneer in the faith in my own way, in my own time, in the name of God the Father, Son, and Holy Spirit. Amen.

## Meditation 8

# Saint Kevin of Glendalough: Care of Creation

*Theme:* Saint Kevin of Glendalough was an Irish hermit whose life of prayer was manifest in his care and tenderness for all God's creatures. Saint Kevin's life leads us to perceive the divine design of the created order; we are led to see the harmony God has created and ordained. We also find in Kevin's life stories of intense prayer and chosen hardships, stories of a man whose passion sometimes led him to extreme measures.

*Opening prayer:*

> It were as easy for Jesu
> To renew the withered tree
> As to wither the new
> Were it His will so to do.
> Jesu! Jesu! Jesu!

Jesu! meet it were to praise Him.
There is no plant in the ground
But is full of His virtue,
There is no form in the strand
But is full of His blessing.
Jesu! Jesu! Jesu!
Jesu! meet it were to praise Him.
There is no life in the sea,
There is no creature in the river,
There is naught in the firmament,
But proclaims His goodness.
Jesu! Jesu! Jesu!
Jesu! meet it were to praise Him.
There is no bird on the wing,
There is no star in the sky,
There is nothing beneath the sun,
But proclaims His goodness.
Jesu! Jesu! Jesu!
Jesu! meet it were to praise Him.

(*Carmina Gadelica,* p. 45)

## About Kevin

Kevin of Glendalough was born in Ireland in the sixth century. Of royal lineage, Kevin was heralded by an angel, who told his mother that the infant would be "dear to both God and man." From an early age, Kevin was known to be a gifted young man, called by God. He studied with three holy monks, yet continued to feel a desire to live as a hermit. One day he ran away into the Wicklow Mountains (south of modern Dublin), and there he came upon the valley of Glendalough (Glen of the Two Lakes). After spending some time there, he returned to the monastery of his teachers. His desire to live as a hermit never left him. Though he founded the monastic city of Glendalough, Kevin's deepest call was to live apart, in the company of wild creatures, offering prayer and sacrifice to the living God. He sought the presence of God in wild places, apart from human society. Nevertheless, Kevin was a soul friend to both humans and animals.

One day after Kevin had retired to his hermit's cell, he was praying the psalms using his Psalter. Lost in prayer, he dropped the precious book into the water of the upper lake. Kevin was distraught; the book was dear to him. As he lamented his loss, an otter retrieved the Psalter from the bottom of the lake and brought it to him. Though the book had been immersed, not one letter was smudged, nor any page ruined.

The tradition tells us that this same otter had the custom of taking salmon to the monks at the monastery on the lake from time to time. Eventually one of the monks decided to kill the otter so he could sell its pelt. The otter discerned this and no longer brought salmon to the monks. The monks then became hungry and left the monastery. Upon hearing about the otter's disappearance, Kevin prayed that he might know the reason for it, and soon the monk who had intended to kill the otter went to Kevin and confessed.

Kevin prayed deeply and often. He prayed rigorously, sometimes going to the icy waters of the lake with his arms outstretched in a cruciform stance. During Lent he would lie on flagstones with his arms outstretched in this same cruciform way. One time when he was praying, hands outstretched, a blackbird landed in his open palm and began to make her nest. Kevin, out of deference to the bird's need, kept his arms outstretched, though they ached with pain. He kept his palm still until the blackbird's fledglings grew old enough to fly.

Kevin's story is filled with incidents of tender encounters with wild creatures. He befriended a wolf, an otter, a wild boar, and other creatures. Yet his life also manifested his chosen asceticism in prayer, which led to his personal deprivation. He, like John the Baptist, dressed in animal skins. He lived on a diet of herbs and water and slept on the rocks surrounding the lakes. Although Kevin's passion for God resulted in extreme practices in prayer, these practices did not take precedence over the need of the smallest creature.

*Pause:* How has the presence of God been revealed to you in wild creatures?

## Kevin's Words

"All the wild creatures on these mountains are my house mates, gentle and familiar with me."

(Waddell, p. 119)

## Reflection

Kevin's guiding presence in prayer calls us to see each creature as an expression of Christ's own goodness and love. Kevin's life is the story of a man willing to put down his own needs and desires in order to serve the blackbird and the otter. Kevin teaches us to honor all creation as God's own handiwork, and to see every aspect of creation as evidence of the divine presence and care. Kevin allows the creatures their own dignity and grace, and interacts with them as co-inhabitors of God's intricately ordered world.

- Saint Kevin left his monastery to dwell in his hermitage in solitude; his life manifests a desire to honor his deepest affection for God. All of us have hidden yearnings for God, some of which we know well, some of which may move within us in sighs too deep for words. Allow yourself to be still and relaxed. What do you yearn for from the living God? Perhaps you yearn for a growing sense of God's presence. Perhaps you have a hidden hunger for God's wisdom. Tell God one of your deepest yearnings. Then hold that yearning in prayer. Thank God for hearing you, and ask for help in knowing how your prayer is being answered.

- In the Celtic tradition, many of the saints were hermits. They lived solitary lives, often in deserted places. Many of these saints had tender relationships with wild animals. The animals were known as co-hermits, creatures who shared the solitude of the saint and in some cases taught the saint patience, kindness, care, or wisdom. Recall an animal, a wild creature or perhaps a pet, that has been a friend and a companion to you. Give thanks for the life of that creature. If possible, perform a concrete act of mercy for that creature as a sign of Christ's love for all beings.

- The Celtic Christian tradition very strongly proclaims that the world is God's and is full of God's glory. The created order is seen as interdependent, all created beings coming from the same holy Source. Traditionally, Celtic Christians would pray the following on the night of the new moon:

> He Who created thee
> Created me likewise;
> He who gave thee weight and light
> Gave to me life and death.
>
> (*Carmina Gadelica*, p. 290)

Practice saying this prayer upon seeing the variety of creation—the sun, the stars, the trees, the wildflowers, the clouds, the sea, the animals, the birds. As your eye beholds the created order, pray with each beholding, "He Who created thee created me likewise." Make notes in your journal describing changes in your awareness.

- In Kevin's story we are given an example of a saint who was connected to the natural world. Many of us find ourselves living in cities surrounded by buildings and asphalt, drawing our water from faucets and our light from a switch. Kevin and many other Celtic saints lead us to an awareness of our dependence on the fabric of God's created order for our existence. Pray for the health of our planet, for the cleansing of water, air, and soil. Pray for the particular ecological concerns in your hometown or city, in your state, and in your country.

## God's Word

> Oil to make a cheerful countenance,*
> and bread to strengthen the heart.
> The trees of the Lord are full of sap,*
> the cedars of Lebanon which he planted,
> In which the birds build their nests,*
> and in whose tops the stork makes his dwelling.
> The high hills are a refuge for the mountain goats,*
> and the stony cliffs for the rock badgers.
> You appointed the moon to mark the seasons, *
> and the sun knows the time of its setting.
> You make darkness that it may be night,*
> in which all the beasts of the forest prowl.

The lions roar after their prey*
and seek their food from God.

(P<small>SALM</small> 104:16–22)

*Closing prayer:* Loving God who creates all the creatures that live on the earth, help me to respect each living thing as your handiwork and to live my life in kindness and consideration for the animals whose bodies may feed me, whose skins may clothe me, whose lives grant me companionship and care. Amen.

# Meditation 9

# Saint Ita: The Wisdom of the Indwelling Spirit

*Theme:* Saint Ita, who is often called the foster mother of the saints of Ireland, stands in the tradition of the great wisdom teachers of the Christian faith. The wisdom of her teaching and guidance come from the indwelling of the Holy Trinity. To pray with Ita is to learn to listen to that life within ourselves.

*Opening prayer:*

> May I speak each day according to Thy justice,
> Each day may I show Thy chastening, O God;
> May I speak each day according to Thy Wisdom,
> Each day and night may I be at peace with Thee.
> *(Carmina Gadelica,* p. 48)

## About Ita

Ita was born into a noble Irish family during the sixth century. At a young age, she was drawn by the fire of the Holy Spirit to love the things of God. Her generosity and discipline were unusual for one so young. One night in a dream, an angel appeared to her and offered her three precious stones. When she sought the meaning of this dream, the angel revealed that the stones symbolized the gifts of the Blessed Trinity and that these gifts would guide her throughout her life. Trusting the Holy Spirit, Ita began to listen. Not only did she listen, she prayed and fasted so as to discern more clearly the meaning of her life. As the Holy Spirit taught her, Ita listened.

Ita began to see change and transformation in herself and in those around her. Her father had at first refused her request to dedicate her life to Christ. Ita would not be daunted. She trusted her vocation and trusted that God would open the door for her father to agree. Her trust did not come easily. For three days and nights she prayed, struggling against a desire to give up. She was fervent in prayer, and in the end, even the bedeviling spirit acknowledged that Ita would be set free, and that many others would be set in her keeping. On the same night, an angel appeared to her father and foretold the great service that Ita would offer her people. This convinced her father to grant Ita's request.

Ita's gift of listening to the indwelling Trinity led her to seek a place for her ministry. She was led to Kileedy in County Limerick. Other women soon joined her. Ita became known for the wisdom of her teaching and the power of her prayers in prophecy and healing.

Ita knew that the Holy Spirit was the true teacher, and with that wisdom she established a school for young boys. Many of the boys sent to her came from places far away; she was known as a true foster mother in the faith. One of her most famous foster sons was Brendan the Navigator, best known for his famous voyages.

Saint Ita's greatest wisdom was her adherence to prayer and seeking guidance from the Blessed Trinity. She often retreated to the solitude of her simple hut. In these times she was said to be so near the company of heaven that she became the nursemaid of Christ. Perhaps this was an expression of the intimacy she felt in being so close to the Source of wisdom. When she came forth from prayer to counsel those in distress, her words had great power because she could see the truth in any situation. Each person who came into her presence went away with an experience of the living God.

*Pause:* Reflect on the wisdom that you have received from the indwelling of the Holy Trinity.

## Ita's Words

Three things that please God most are true faith in God with a pure heart, a simple life with a grateful spirit, and generosity inspired by charity. The three things that most displease God are a mouth that hates people, a heart harboring resentments, and confidence in wealth.

(Sellner, p. 154)

## Reflection

Throughout Ita's life, the fullness and wisdom of God's life grew within her. Her life began with desire for and attentiveness to the fine stirrings of the Spirit within her and was strengthened and nurtured by prayer, solitude, and perseverance. The fruits of her life were seen in the wisdom she received and passed on to others.

We too are invited to participate in the life of God and to listen to the wisdom that is revealed to us in the indwelling of the Holy Trinity. It is in our inner life that we often find the true wisdom we need to offer healing, to build community, and to teach with spiritual authority.

- Recall a time when your own teaching or counsel was guided by the wisdom of the Holy Spirit. Did you notice a different quality to your thoughts and your words?

- Jesus is often called the Wisdom of God. In his own time he was most often addressed as *rabbi,* meaning "teacher," for he was recognized as one having authority from heaven. If you have a question in prayer, begin the question with the word *rabbi.*

- Reread Ita's teaching about the three qualities that God loves and the three qualities that displease God. At the moment, which of these qualities does God love in you? How might you now be displeasing God?

- Wisdom comes from many sources. From where do you seek wisdom?
  - solitude
  - spiritual retreats
  - the Scriptures
  - a pilgrimage
  - soul friends
  - God's creation
  - solidarity with the poor and suffering

Recall the voices of wisdom you have heard.

- King Solomon's desire for wisdom was expressed in the hope for a "listening heart" (see 1 KINGS 3:9 NEB). Spend some time in silence listening to the wisdom that comes from silence.

## God's Word

> Does not wisdom call,
> and does not understanding raise her voice?
> On the heights, beside the way,
> at the crossroads she takes her stand;
> beside the gates in front of the town,
> at the entrance of the portals she cries out:
> "To you, O people, I call,
> and my cry is to all that live.
> O simple ones, learn prudence;
> acquire intelligence, you who lack it.
> Hear, for I will speak noble things,
> and from my lips will come what is right;
> for my mouth will utter truth; wickedness is an abomination to my lips."
>
> (PROVERBS 8:1–7)

*Closing prayer:* O Wisdom from on high, come and dwell within me, that my life might be wise, patterned by your life. Amen.

# Meditation 10

# Saint Brendan the Navigator: Holy Journeying

*Theme:* The life of Saint Brendan is a story of adventure and risk, of sailing forth on uncharted waters, responding to the call of the Holy One. From Brendan we learn that God accompanies us at every moment of our life journey and calls us forth in trust and faith.

*Opening prayer:*

> Be Thou a smooth way before me,
> Be Thou a guiding star above me,
> Be Thou a keen eye behind me,
> This day, this night, for ever.
> I am weary, and I forlorn,
> Lead Thou me to the land of the angels;
> Methinks it were time I went for a space
> To the court of Christ, to the peace of heaven.
> If only Thou, O God of life,

Be at peace with me, be my support,
Be to me as a star, be to me as a helm
From my lying down in peace to my rising anew.

(Carmina Gadelica, p. 241)

## About Brendan

Brendan the Navigator was born near modern-day Tralee in western Ireland in 486. His birth was signaled by angelic presences heralding the coming of a child who would be dedicated to Christ. Owing to these signals of a saintly destiny, Brendan was, at an early age, placed under the foster care of Saint Ita. He learned the Old and New Testaments and studied the monastic rules of Ireland. He discerned at an early age that he was called to become a priest. At his ordination, these words from the gospel proved to be prophetic: "Truly I tell you, there is no one who has left house or brothers or sisters or mother or father or children or fields, for my sake and for the sake of the good news, who will not receive a hundredfold now in this age" (MARK 10:29–30a). Brendan's life was characterized by a willingness to sail to new lands for Christ, risking life and limb upon the swelling ocean as holy journeys led him far away from his home.

Brendan's love for his Lord proved greater than his love for his homeland. Like many other Celtic saints, Brendan left what was known and well-loved. Departing from family, friends, and home, Brendan and twelve other monks undertook what became known as the "white martyrdom." They began voyaging, hoping to discover the Land of the Saints, the place where no human blood had ever been shed. As reported in the *Book of Lismore,* Brendan "sailed then with some chosen men over the wave-voice of the strong-maned sea, and over the storm of the green-sided waves, and over the mouths of the marvellous, awful, bitter, ocean" (Marsh and Bamford, p. 81).

The boats used by the Celtic saints were called coracles. These small vessels were made by stretching animal skins across a wooden frame and sealing the seams with pitch. Many stories from this tradition tell of persons getting into a coracle without oars, trusting the current of a river or the ocean to guide them to "the place of resurrection." Such acts of trust in God's guidance and providence were carried out again and again, and serve as a reminder that when we entrust ourselves to God's guidance, we will be carried to a holy dying and a holy rising.

Brendan and his fellow monks had many adventures as they sailed the sea. At one point they discovered that the rock they had landed on to celebrate the Easter feast was actually a whale (itself a symbol of resurrection from the Book of Jonah). They spent seven years on the sea, often marveling at the wonders of creation and continually being thankful that God provided for their needs.

After the sea voyage, Brendan helped establish a monastic community at Clonfert, which he called his "place of resurrection." As he was dying, he asked that he be buried at that place, where he had known community and where his days of holy journeying had led him.

*Pause:* In what ways has the living God accompanied you on the journey of your life?

## Brendan's Words

Beloved brothers, I am asking your advice and help, for my heart and thoughts are fixed on one single desire, if

it be God's desire, and that is to seek the land . . . God
has promised to those who come after us.

(Sellner, p. 60)

## Reflection

Brendan's story gives us an example of a man willing to trust
God enough to venture into unknown waters regardless of the
risk of deadly failure. The metaphor of journey is often used for
the spiritual life. As we grow in the life of prayer, we learn more
about trust, hope, and God's providential care and guidance.

- How do you feel about going to places that are unknown to
  you? What experiences have you had of being led to a new
  place and discovering that God has led you there? Thank
  God for accompanying you and guiding you.

- In the Celtic tradition is this saying about pilgrimage:

    To go to Rome
    Is much trouble, little profit.
    The King whom thou seekest there,
    Unless thou bring Him with thee, thou wilt not find.
    (Allchin and de Waal, *Daily Readings,* p. 74)

When we pray with Brendan, we are taught by his
example. We learn that finding Christ is not just the goal of
our journey—Christ is our companion on the way. We may
be aware of Christ's presence in our life journey in many
ways—through friends, through loneliness that only Christ
can fill, through surprise encounters that gift us with new-
ness. Reflect on your activities of the last week. In what

ways have you known Christ's accompanying presence? How have you thanked him for his friendship?

- When one embarks on a pilgrimage, what happens along the way may be surprising and unexpected. What has happened to you in the last week that has come unexpectedly? Was the unexpected good news? What were your responses to these unknowns? What did you discover about your ability to trust?

- The Celtic Christian tradition emphatically declares the goodness of our created life. This tradition also perceives death as another birth, as a moment of moving from an earthly reality to an eternal one. When the Celtic saints set off in their coracles, trusting their lives to the current of God's love, they were always seeking the place of resurrection, the place where their dying and rising to new life would occur. They were clear minded and trusting about mortality, and sensed that the daily act of trusting God allowed them to practice for the ultimate entrusting that comes at the end of our days. Have you ever reflected on your own dying? What feelings, fears, sadnesses, and joys come to mind? When you reach your place of resurrection, what sort of person would you like to be?

## God's Word

> Lord, you have searched me out and known me;*
> you know my sitting down and my rising up;
> you discern my thoughts from afar.
> You trace my journeys and my resting-places*
> and are acquainted with all my ways.

Indeed, there is not a word on my lips,*
but you, O Lord, know it altogether.
You press upon me behind and before*
and lay your hand upon me.
Such knowledge is too wonderful for me;*
it is so high that I cannot attain to it.
Where can I go then from your Spirit?*
where can I flee from your presence?
If I climb up to heaven, you are there;*
if I make the grave my bed, you are there also.
If I take the wings of the morning*
and dwell in the uttermost parts of the sea,
Even there your hand will lead me*
and your right hand hold me fast.

(PSALM 139:1–9)

*Closing prayer:* Dear Friend and Companion in my life journey, you are with me wherever I go. Grant me the eyes to see your faithful and gracious presence, that I may seek your guidance and entrust myself to your loving care each day. Amen.

# Meditation 11

# Saint Illtyd of Wales: Perseverance

*Theme:* In the life of Saint Illtyd of Wales, we have an example of a persevering follower of Christ. Saint Illtyd manifested qualities of loyalty, dedication, and discipline throughout his life, and became the spiritual father of many of the faithful in Wales.

*Opening prayer:*

> Holy God, loving Father, of the word everlasting,
> Grant me to have of Thee this living prayer:
> Lighten my understanding, kindle my will, begin my doing,
> Incite my love, strengthen my weakness, enfold my desire.
> Cleanse my heart, make holy my soul, confirm my faith,
> Keep safe my mind and compass my body about;
> As I utter my prayer from my mouth,
> In mine own heart may I feel Thy presence.
>
> *(Carmina Gadelica,* p. 207)

## About Illtyd

Saint Illtyd lived during the fifth century in Wales. We know that he began his adult life as a soldier. Some legends say that he was one of the knights of King Arthur's court. He spent his early life engaging in combat, as ordered by his commanding officer.

After some years Saint Illtyd discerned that he could no longer live as a soldier. One account relates that his company of soldiers unwittingly rode into a swamp and drowned. Another story credits Saint Cadog, also a soldier who became a monk, with fostering Saint Illtyd's conversion. In any case, Illtyd began to desire to live a holy life, a life dedicated fully to Christ. He received an angelic message that told him where to build his monastery in Glamorgan. He followed these heavenly orders after having made his confession to the local bishop and receiving absolution.

Saint Illtyd built his monastic house outside the modern-day city of Cardiff at a place known as Llanilltud Fawr. There he created a great center of learning and formation, a place where many came to study and to become dedicated to the gospel of Christ. The soldier who had known how to take orders and how to carry them out became a deeply dedicated follower of Christ. His life and his erudition were naturally attractive to many who sought to become sincere disciples. Saint David of Wales, among many others, received his learning from Saint Illtyd's community.

Though learning and prayer were central to Saint Illtyd's life, he is often depicted with a plow. Tradition says he introduced a new technique for plowing fields, which was adopted throughout the countryside.

Saint Illtyd's innovative method of plowing is indicative of his willingness to persevere—in learning, in prayer, in discipleship, in the tilling of the land. The earliest known document about Illtyd refers to him as the most learned of all the Britons in the knowledge of Scripture, both the Old Testament and the New Testament, and in every branch of philosophy—poetry and rhetoric, grammar and arithmetic; and he was most sagacious and gifted with the power of foretelling future events (Doble, p. 88).

Illtyd is a model of perseverance, and to the end of his days, he continued to learn and impart what he had learned, whether the knowledge was about the Scriptures or about agriculture. He was truly generous with the wisdom and knowledge he acquired, and always persevered in his desire to continue to deepen and broaden in Christ.

*Pause:* In what ways have you had to persevere? How has the need to persevere changed you?

## Illtyd's Words

On the day he died, Illtyd addressed his brother monks:

> I rejoice, dearest brethren, that you have come, because the time is at hand that I should depart and fall asleep in Christ, and you shall duly honour me . . . But be of good cheer . . . I indeed shall be received tonight by the hands of angels, about midnight, in the presence of you all.
>
> (Doble, p. 89)

## Reflection

In Saint Illtyd's life we see the example of one who perseveres, to the end of his days. He apparently had a deeply felt desire for learning and for inviting others to learn, and this desire shaped his life. Through perseverance he created a monastic center that was truly a light in the midst of darkness. At a time when the old order of the Roman Empire was being destroyed and much valuable knowledge was at risk of being lost, Saint Illtyd founded Llanilltud Fawr. Persevering in times that were bleak and violent, he brought forth a community that encouraged learning and discipleship.

- Saint Illtyd desired to learn throughout his life. What desires has God placed in your heart that may shape your life? How do you perceive the ways those desires have already changed your lifestyle? Thank God for the desires that are God-given, and ask for a blessing upon them.

- Saint Illtyd was a soldier before he became an abbot. Some of the qualities of his life as a soldier helped him in his life as an abbot—loyalty and obedience, for example. Though his life as an abbot was very different from his life as a soldier, some continuity existed between one life and the other. Reflect on your own life at present. What qualities in yourself do you hope to nurture in Christ throughout all your days? What qualities need transformation? What qualities help you to persevere during hardship or uncertainty?

- At Saint Illtyd's church in Llantwit Major in south Wales, a visitor finds remnants of Celtic crosses dating from the seventh century. An ancient baptismal font, marked with Celtic designs, stands near the crosses. This part of the church is built on the site of Saint Illtyd's fifth-century monastery. A visitor gazing at these treasures of the church will also notice the memorial plaques on the walls, dedicated to the faithful from this parish who have died over the centuries. To the east stands the sanctuary where the worshiping community of today gathers to offer praise and thanksgiving. The perseverance of Saint Illtyd has borne the fruit of a persevering community of the baptized.

Where have you encountered this sort of persevering faith? Who were the people who demonstrated persevering faith to you? What did you learn from their example? Give thanks for their lives and for the fruit they have borne.

- Saint Illtyd's pupils included Saint David, Saint Samson, and Saint Gildas, all of whom were important to the life of the church in Wales in those early years. Saint Illtyd's monastic school became a place of encouragement and formation, of seeking and prayer. What places have given you encouragement in your Christian life? What places have helped you learn and grow? Give thanks for those places, for the teachers, and for your fellow learners. If you feel it is appropriate, write a note of thanksgiving to one of your mentors.

## God's Word

*Beloved, I do not consider that I have made it my own; but this one thing I do: forgetting what lies behind and straining forward to what lies ahead, I press on toward the goal for the prize of the heavenly call of God in Christ Jesus.*

(PHILIPPIANS 3:13–14)

*Closing prayer:* All my life begins and ends in you, loving God. Grant me the grace to continue to grow in you, that at the end of my days, I will rejoice to have persevered. Amen.

## Meditation 12

# Saint Winefride of Wales: Wounds and Healing

*Theme:* Saint Winefride's story is one of dying and rising, of being wounded and being healed. The grievous violence that was inflicted on her was transformed; the wounding became a source of healing. Her life manifests the abundantly flowing water of life that heals, transforms, and makes new and beautiful.

*Opening prayer:*

> Thou, my soul's Healer,
> Keep me at even,
> Keep me at morning,
> Keep me at noon,
> On rough course faring,
> Help and safeguard
> My means this night.
> I am tired, astray, and stumbling,
> Shield Thou me from snare and sin.
>
> (*Carmina Gadelica,* p. 215)

## About Winefride

Much of the tradition that we have received about the life of
Saint Winefride is the stuff of legend. We are told that from the
tender years of childhood, she felt a strong attraction to her
Lord, and desired deeply to lead a holy life. She began to study
with her uncle, Saint Beuno, and to learn Scripture. Her family
supported her call to prayer. Winefride was also known for her
beauty—the sort of beauty that is both without and within.

One day a local prince, Caradog, saw Winefride and was
immediately seized with a desire to have her as his own. He did
not fall in love; he was overcome by lust. He saw Winefride as a
possession to be obtained, as a woman to be taken. He began to
seek her company, which she courteously refused. Her refusal
inspired him to a more ferocious lust. When yet again she declined
his advances, he charged after her in rage. She ran from him but
was cornered. Caradog, furious that he could not have her, struck
at her with his sword, cleaving her head from her body.

In the ensuing turmoil and confusion, Winefride's uncle,
Saint Beuno, came upon the scene. We are told that he immediately knelt, replaced her severed head, and prayed for
Christ's healing. Winefride was restored to life, and from the
ground where her blood was spilled, a holy well immediately
sprang up, a well gushing with water granted for life and for
healing. Saint Beuno then confronted Caradog, saying, "I ask God
not to spare you and to respect you as little as you respected
this girl." One version of the story tells us that Caradog melted
away into a lake and was seen no more.

Once healed, Winefride took vows and began her consecrated life. She established a community of women, which pos-
sibly became a double monastery where both men and women
sought to lead a vowed monastic life.

*Pause:* How have you experienced healing of body, mind, and spirit?

## Poetry about Winefride

We have no surviving words or quotations attributed to Winefride, but the great Jesuit poet Gerard Manley Hopkins wrote about her in his poem "The Leaden Echo and the Golden Echo."

> Give beauty back, beauty, beauty, beauty, back to God,
> beauty's self and beauty's giver.
> See; not a hair is, not an eyelash, not the least lash lost;
> every hair
> Is, hair of the head, numbered.

> (In Gardner, p. 54)

## Reflection

Though Winefride's story is replete with the characteristics of legend, therein we find this truth: the power of the risen Christ may heal all wounds, and that healing reveals God's beautiful mercy at work in us. Winefride endured the wounds of being seen as an object to be possessed. She was violated by Caradog's gaze and overpowered by his actions. She suffered the ultimate wound of being killed. Yet through prayer she was made new. Winefride's life calls us to remember that as we seek to walk in our Lord's path of life, we may be wounded by those who do not understand or who are antagonistic and violent.

Winefride's story also leads us to become wounded healers. Praying with Winefride allows us to acknowledge our own wounds and to ask for their healing, that the water of life may flow through us to others. A particular beauty of spirit comes through those who have offered their wounds to Christ and have received his healing.

- Winefride's life reveals a singular desire to serve the risen Christ. She came from a family that recognized her vocation, supported her, helped her to grow and study. Who in your life has served as your spiritual parent? Who has supported and encouraged the growing life of Christ within you? Give thanks for each person, naming him or her and recalling the moments when you have been supported in your life in Christ.

- Who have you known who has manifested beauty of spirit? How have they been a healing presence for you? What have you learned from their example? Make a prayer ribbon from a long strip of paper. Write the names of the persons who occur to you on the paper. Then drape it in a tree or shrub, allowing the elements to receive your prayer. (This practice is followed to this day at many of the holy wells throughout Ireland and Wales.)

- Holywell, the site in north Wales sacred to Saint Winefride, is still visited by pilgrims. At Holywell, an artesian spring gushes up, an estimated twenty-four tons of water welling up to the surface every minute. The water comes forth beautifully clear and sparkling, abundantly appearing from the depths of the earth. Around the spring, pilgrims seeking healing of body, mind, and spirit pray and bathe themselves with the water. There is a meeting of deep need and abundant water, symbolic of God's never-ending grace, which is more than we can imagine.

  Reflect for a moment on instances when you have experienced God's abundance. What feelings came to you?

How was God's abundance made known to you? What healing did you experience in knowing God's abundance?

• Saint Winefride is often depicted with a fountain at her feet and a red ring around her neck—the scar from her wounding. In her life the scar becomes both a sign of the wounding and a sign of the healing. The red ring connects her both to Caradog, the agent of the violence, and to Saint Beuno, who served as an instrument of grace.

Perhaps you bear scars, either in the flesh or in the soul, that recall both a wounding and a healing. What stories do those scars tell? Write down one of these stories. Allow yourself to write the truth of the wounding; allow yourself to receive the grace and beauty of the ongoing healing. Give thanks for those who were agents of healing in your life; ask for the grace to forgive any agents of wounding.

• In Winefride's story, we encounter not only wounding but dying. Caradog's ferocity and lust lead him to cut off Winefride's head. One way to relate to this part of the story is to reflect on difficult times, times when we have felt cut off from our deepest selves. Perhaps a situation at home, at work, or in some social group has led us to be cut off from the desires that come from Christ. This is one form of spiritual death. Being cut off from our true selves in Christ leads us to live inauthentically, and on occasion to live in a way that hurts ourselves or others.

Have you experienced a time of being cut off from your true self in Christ? What did that feel like? How did you know when it was time to move from dying to rising? What helped you make the transition from dying to rising? What did you learn from that transition?

## God's Word

> I will exalt you, O Lord,
> because you have lifted me up*
> and have not let my enemies triumph over me.
> O Lord my God, I cried out to you,*
> and you restored me to health.
> You brought me up, O Lord, from the dead;*
> you restored my life as I was going down to the grave.
> Sing to the Lord, you servants of his;*
> give thanks for the remembrance of his holiness.
> For his wrath endures but the twinkling of an eye,*
> his favor for a lifetime.
>
> (PSALM 30:1–5)

*Closing prayer:* In all my woundings and all my healings, in all my dyings and all my risings, be with me, living God, to mend and restore, to heal and make whole. Amen.

# Meditation 13

# Saint Aidan: Generosity

*Theme:* Saint Aidan has been called a true apostle, for by the generosity of his words and actions, many lives were touched by the gospel of Jesus Christ. To pray with Aidan is to be open to God's generosity flowing in and through us.

*Opening prayer:*

Each thing I have received, from Thee it came,
Each thing for which I hope, from Thy love it will come.
Each thing I enjoy, it is of Thy bounty,
Each thing I am, comes of Thy disposing.
And grant Thou to me, Father beloved,
From Whom each thing that is freely flows,
That no tie over-strict, no tie over-dear
May be between myself and this world below.
(Carmina Gadelica, p. 207)

## About Aidan

Aidan was an Irishman by birth, but spent his formative years as a monk on the island of Iona off Scotland. There he learned the values of prayer, study, self-discipline, and almsgiving that were to shape his future ministry.

At the time Aidan lived on the island, King Oswald of Northumbria sent to Iona for a bishop to come and teach the Christian faith to all his subjects. The monk who was sent first returned to Iona frustrated and angry, saying the people of Northumbria were unteachable and barbaric. As the elders of Iona gathered to consider their next plan, Aidan stood up and suggested that people who had never heard the gospel needed to learn of it gradually, and that the monks' approach as evangelists should be gentle. Sensing in Aidan a spirit of humility and practical wisdom, the elders consecrated him as a bishop and missionary to the Saxons.

Aidan arrived in Northumbria in 635 and set up his foundation on the isle of Lindisfarne, which would become known as Holy Island. He knew from the beginning that he would need an isolated place for solitude and prayer to prepare for the great demands of his mission. He also knew that he would need the generosity of King Oswald, who would provide the resources for Aidan's ministry as well as the translation of the gospel into the native language of the Saxons.

Aidan's ministry could be symbolized by an outstretched hand. He liked to walk among the people. To the unbelievers he brought the hope of belief. To the newly converted he taught the value of prayer and Scripture. He encouraged them in generosity and acts of mercy. He demonstrated this in his own life, always aware of and quick to respond to the needs of the poor. For those bound by slavery, he found the means to freedom, and later provided for their instruction on the isle of Lindisfarne.

Stories have been passed down that tell of Aidan's great delight in giving away gifts he had received. In one story the king gave Aidan a fine horse laden with royal trappings. Aidan graciously received the horse. However, upon seeing a poor beggar on the road, Aidan dismounted and gave the horse to the poor man. When the king heard the story, he was clearly perturbed, and questioned harshly Aidan's judgment in giving away such a valuable gift. Aidan responded: "King, what are you saying? Surely that son of a mare is not dearer to you than that son of God." Aidan's humble yet prophetic voice brought the king back to the truth of the gospel.

Aidan's life was his message. He withdrew every Lent to Lindisfarne to pray and fast and draw near to the source of his generosity. Even in prayer he was able to see the sufferings of the world and offer hope, generosity, and protection. Once, when a priest and his companions were traveling, Aidan could see that a dangerous storm was about to threaten their safety. His prayers protected them on their journey. Another time, he sensed the danger of an enemy attack on the king and his castle. He prayed fervently for their protection, and his prayers were answered.

Aidan died in the year 651, but his spirit and life continue to inspire the hundreds of pilgrims who still come to the island of Lindisfarne. Presently the Saint Aidan's Trust carries on the apostolic tradition of holiness, simplicity, and generosity of this gentle yet powerful saint.

*Pause:* Reflect on the goodness that comes when you have yielded totally to God.

## Aidan's Words

It seems to me, brother, that you have been unduly severe with your ignorant hearers. You should have followed the guidance of the apostle and offered them at first the milk of simpler teaching, until gradually, growing strong on the food of God's word, they could take in a fuller statement of the faith and carry out God's more exalted commands.

(Marsden, p. 59)

## Reflection

In the life of Aidan we see the zeal and the spirit of the first Apostles, who freely passed on the gifts of grace that they themselves had received from an encounter with the living Christ. The generosity that arises from a life totally dedicated to sharing God's generosity has great power to transform the world.

Spiritual giving does not demand something be given in return. It is not a giving that objectifies the one receiving, nor is it a giving that merely fills a void in the giver. It is a response to the true giver of life, a giving as Christ gives.

The power of generosity is that it intuitively listens to another's deepest needs. The listener then responds concretely and specifically to those needs. We see Jesus healing the sick, feeding the hungry, calming those who are afraid. Saint Aidan continues in the spirit of Christ by teaching the lost ones and providing for the poor. To pray in this spirit leads us to experience the steady stream of God's love flowing through us, leading us to the places that are most in need of such love.

- Deep gratitude lies at the heart of Celtic prayer. A grateful heart is the beginning of generosity. Reflect on the events of your last twenty-four hours. In what moment did you feel the most grateful? What does that moment teach you about what is most important in your life? Express your gratitude to God for the gift of the moment.

- Generosity implies a gift given without conditions. The first monk sent from Iona to Northumbria was unable to give freely because he expected a specific response. When the receivers could not meet his expectations, he withdrew in anger and resentment.
    - Bring to mind someone who needs your generosity but is unable to receive what you have to offer.
    - Picture the person in your mind.
    - Express to God your desires and hopes for that person.
    - Express also your frustrations and disappointments.
    - Picture that person surrounded by God's generosity, receiving all the good gifts that God has stored up for that person.
    - Rest in the assurance that God's generosity is even greater than our own.

- Our inclination to give or to withhold is often reflected in the language of our body. Sit in a comfortable chair with your feet flat on the floor. Place your hands on your lap and make a tight fist. As you hold your fist tightly, pray these words: "Here I am, Lord. Send me." How does your body affect the meaning of your prayer? Now open your hands. Place them palms up on your lap, and pray the same words. Do you notice a difference? Sit for a moment in openness to the Spirit.

- Aidan's generosity was often concrete and specific to each person. He did not want to be aloof from the people, so he walked among them and saw their needs. As you begin this day, prepare to meet one person prayerfully and intentionally with the eyes of Christ. This may cause you to make a specific response. At the end of the day, recall that person and notice any changes in your reaction to that person. Imagine the reality of approaching every person with these eyes.

- Great freedom can be found in a radical act of generosity, such as Aidan's giving away his royal horse. Imagine yourself doing one radical act of generosity. What fears might you confront as you do it? What reactions might you feel from others? How might you feel after having done it? Is Christ calling you to practice a more radical generosity?

## God's Word

*How does God's love abide in anyone who has the world's goods and sees a brother or sister in need and yet refuses help? Little children, let us love, not in word or speech, but in truth and action.*
(1 JOHN 3:17–18)

*Closing prayer:* Gracious God, you have blessed us with the gift of life. Each day your generosity is showered on us in countless acts of mercy. May your generosity flow through us so that all people everywhere may know the richness of your love. Amen.

## Meditation 14

# Saint Cuthbert of Lindisfarne: Holy Gentleness

*Theme:* Saint Cuthbert's life manifests the gentle and wise presence of Christ. Cuthbert was known far and wide for his gentleness, his hospitality, and his tender mercy to both creatures and people. His life guides us to pray for the gentle presence of Christ in our speech, our actions, our life.

*Opening prayer:*

> Thanks to Thee, O ever gentle Christ,
> That Thou hast raised me freely from the black
> And from the darkness of last night
> To the kindly light of this day.
> Praise unto Thee, O God of all creatures,
> According to each life Thou hast poured on me,
> My desire, my word, my sense, my repute,
> My thought, my deed, my way, my fame.
>
> (*Carmina Gadelica,* p. 198)

## About Cuthbert

Saint Cuthbert, who lived in the seventh century, came from a family that lived in the northernmost reaches of England or southern Scotland. As a young boy, Cuthbert was tending sheep one night when he saw angels carrying a holy soul to heaven. Later he discovered that Saint Aidan of Lindisfarne had died that night. This discovery led Cuthbert to vow that he would follow in Aidan's footsteps, dedicating himself to the spread of the gospel in Northumbria. The lives of Saint Aidan and Saint Cuthbert were thereafter linked, for Cuthbert would eventually come to be abbot of Lindisfarne.

Cuthbert was a gifted preacher and teacher who had a strength and gentleness that drew people to his message. His life embodied the gentleness of Christ; therefore, the words he spoke sprang from an inner spirit of mercy and kindness.

Cuthbert was drawn to solitude, but he often interrupted his times of isolation with times of active leadership. He became an abbot and a bishop, both roles requiring him to be engaged in administration, decision making, and church deliberations. His gentle presence was also marked by his courage to speak the truth of the gospel and to be a reconciler when factions began to contend with one another. Cuthbert lived at a time when the mission of the church in Rome, which was based at Canterbury in the south, and the mission of Ireland and Iona, which came from the north, didn't always agree. Though formed by the practice of the Celtic monks, Cuthbert sought unity and peace in the church.

In these times of active leadership, Cuthbert's gift of holy gentleness allowed him to lead as Christ leads—from an inner authority and wisdom. Cuthbert's desire for solitude allowed him to cultivate these inherent qualities. On the island of Lindisfarne, which twice a day is cut off from the mainland by the action of the tides, Cuthbert sought the greater solitude of a little prayer cell on the Inner Farne. This more isolated island had no water, no food, and no trees. The monks carved a well from rock so that Cuthbert might have water and brought seeds to be sown even though the soil was thin. Here among the elements, surrounded by the eider ducks and sea otters, Cuthbert devoted himself to even deeper prayer and listening, offering his life as living prayer.

Cuthbert often prayed at night. He would stand in the cold sea with his arms extended, his body resembling a cross. According to one legend, he had prayed in the sea for hours one night, and as he walked ashore, two otters came to him and dried his feet with their fur.

Even at Inner Farne, seekers came to Cuthbert for counsel and wisdom. Known for his Christlike qualities, Cuthbert naturally drew others to himself. The "ever gentle Christ" showed forth in him; a holy presence called him to be an offering to God.

Cuthbert died on Lindisfarne and was buried there. In the late eighth century, Viking raids forced the monks to leave Lindisfarne, but they took Cuthbert's body with them. The "Cuthbert folk," as they were called, journeyed throughout northern England, keeping the saint's body safe from invaders. Finally Cuthbert was brought to rest at Durham. In 995 a church was built to house his remains, which were later placed behind the altar of Durham Cathedral.

*Pause:* When have you experienced gentleness?

## Cuthbert's Words

Live in mutual harmony with all other servants of
Christ. Do not despise those faithful who come to you
seeking hospitality. Receive them, put them up, and set
them on their way with kindness, treating them as one
of yourselves. Do not ever think yourselves better than
the rest of your companions who share the same faith
and follow the monastic life.

(Sellner, p. 111)

## Reflection

Even when he sought deeper solitude, Cuthbert demonstrated
the gift of gentle hospitality. From his little oratory on Inner
Farne, he offered the hearth of his shelter and the warmth of
his soul. Hospitality and gentleness often go hand in hand; an
aggressive personality may not be capable of creating open
space to receive another.

- How do you offer hospitality? Picture the place in your
  home where you receive those who may need kindness or
  company or gentleness. Now see Christ himself dwelling in
  that place. Ask for his blessing on the place, on you and on
  those who enter, on words spoken.

- When Cuthbert was first studying to become a monk, his
  mentor was Boisil of Melrose Abbey. Cuthbert asked Boisil
  which book he should study, and Boisil instructed him to
  read the Gospel of Saint John. They studied that book
  together and read a commentary as well. Which book of the
  Bible is your favorite? When was the last time you read that

book all the way through, from beginning to end? Have you had a teacher who helped you study that particular book? What did you learn about yourself? About God? About the calling you may have in your life? If you desire, carefully read that book of the Bible again, paying particular attention to what you learn anew.

- On the isle of Lindisfarne, the ebb and flow of the tides rhythmically connect and separate the isle from the mainland. At times one can walk from the mainland to the isle. At other times the sea swells and it becomes impossible to reach the mainland on foot. Those residing on the isle thus live in a natural, elemental rhythm that allows for both solitude and connection to the larger sphere of public life.

    In the practice of the Celtic church, this kind of natural rhythm of solitude and community was regularly lived out. On occasion one member of a community would feel the call to live apart and would retire to a little cell to listen and to pray. Then the time for solitude would come to its natural end and the person would be drawn back into the life of community, renewed and refreshed. This pattern was allowed to ebb and flow without rigidity.

    Reflect on the pattern of solitude and community. What is ebbing for you at present? What is flowing? Are you feeling a growing desire for public service, for engagement with others, for active ministry? Are you feeling more drawn to quiet, to reflection, to stillness? Write down what you notice in yourself as you reflect on this. Where do you feel a pull? Notice where your own inner tide is flowing. Without making any judgments, gently note where the shifts are happening.

- Cuthbert's life story includes very tender encounters with creatures. These stories are not sentimental. Rather, they are stories in which the process of being made new has allowed Cuthbert to be as Christ in the midst of creation. When the sea otters dry his feet, they are recognizing the Christ in Cuthbert and offering their animal selves as friends. Cuthbert also regards the animals with respect and courtesy.

     One story tells of an instance when Cuthbert was hungry and an eagle brought him a salmon. Cuthbert cut the salmon in half and shared it with the great bird. In Cuthbert we see an awareness of the interdependence of all things and an acute sense of the intrinsic holiness of all that is created. The animals seem to know that he will not harm them, for he has a reverence for all life.

     Take a moment to look at the creation outside your window. Notice what is there. Write down all the different forms of life that you can see, including everything from grass to beetles to birds. Now slowly pray for each species on your list.

     What insights come to you? Are there any changes in the way you see or experience God's presence?

## God's Word

*We were gentle among you, like a nurse tenderly caring for her own children. So deeply do we care for you that we are determined to share with you not only the gospel of God but also our own selves, because you have become very dear to us.*

(1 THESSALONIANS 2:7–8)

*Closing Prayer:* Ever gentle Christ, grant me the grace to pattern my life like yours, that I may care for your creatures and for my neighbors with your tender care and mercy. Amen.

# Saint Hilda of Whitby: Encouragement

*Theme:* Saint Hilda, the great abbess of Whitby, exemplifies the fruitfulness of a life given to encouragement and empowerment of others. Encouragement inspires us to honor our gifts and to offer them for the life of the world. Encouragement also sustains us in difficult times and brings hope that in God, we will not be overcome.

*Opening prayer:*

> Thanks to be Thee, Jesu Christ,
> For the many gifts Thou hast bestowed on me,
> Each day and night, each sea and land,
> Each weather fair, each calm, each wild.
> I am giving Thee worship with my whole life,
> I am giving Thee assent with my whole power,
> I am giving Thee praise with my whole tongue,
> I am giving Thee honour with my whole utterance.

I am giving Thee love with my whole devotion,
I am giving Thee kneeling with my whole desire,
I am giving Thee love with my whole heart,
I am giving Thee affection with my whole sense;
I am giving Thee my existence with my whole mind,
I am giving Thee my soul, O God of all gods,
My thought, my deed,
My word, my will,
My understanding, my intellect,
My way, my state.

*(Carmina Gadelica,* p. 202)

## About Hilda

Hilda was born into a noble family of Northumbria in 614. She was baptized at an early age by Paulinus and lived a holy, secular life for thirty-three years. Having been educated in the Celtic tradition, she desired to become a nun and to make her pilgrimage to France. However, she was summoned home by Aidan of Lindisfarne to organize communities of faith in various places in Northumbria. Her devotion and wisdom led her to found a double monastery in Whitby, which became known as a center for learning and formation for leaders of the church. Many received Holy Orders at Whitby, including five bishops.

Hilda not only encouraged learning at the monastery but she set up a rule of life that balanced prayer, asceticism, and the sharing of material goods. Her way of living, according to the historical writings of the Venerable Bede, was manifested in justice, holiness, chastity, and especially peace and charity. People from all walks of life and from many regions came to seek Hilda's counsel and encouragement. Her foundation at Whitby was chosen by King Oswy to be the site of a great theological debate, known as the Council of Whitby, between representatives of a mission from Rome and from the Celtic church. Although Hilda was sympathetic to the Celtic church's expression of the faith, she encouraged others to follow the guidance to unite into one church.

Hilda is often remembered for her gift of encouragement to an uneducated herdsman by the name of Caedmon who lived near her monastery. It was said that in the evenings when stories and songs were shared among the community, Caedmon would slip out in embarrassment, returning to the animals he tended, for he had no ability to sing. One night while he was with the animals, he fell asleep and began to dream. In his dream someone called his name, saying, "Caedmon, sing something to me." Caedmon confessed that he didn't know how to sing and for that reason he had left the celebration. The voice then replied, "Sing of the creation." Suddenly Caedmon began to sing beautiful poetry praising God's gift of creation. The next morning he rushed to tell of the gift he had received. Hilda recognized God's grace in his gift and encouraged him to take monastic vows and learn the great stories of the faith. He became a monk and a singer of stories in his native Anglo-Saxon tongue, and is known today as the first English poet.

Hilda's encouragement continued into the last years of her life. She suffered with a lingering illness, yet encouraged those in her charge to give thanks to the Lord in faithfulness. On her deathbed she urged them to be at peace with Christ and with one another.

*Pause:* Reflect on the encouragement you have received and the encouragement you need in order to offer yourself and your gifts wholly to God.

## Hilda's Words

> Trade with the gifts God has given you
> Bend
> your minds to holy learning you
> may escape the fretting moth
> of littleness of mind
> that would wear out
> your souls.
> Brace your wills to action
> that they may not be
> the spoils of weak desires.
> Train your hearts and lips to song
> gives courage to the soul.
> Being buffeted by trials, learn to laugh.
> Being reproved, give thanks.
> Having failed, determine to succeed.
>
> (Maitland and Mulford, p. 106)

## Reflection

A person who encourages others is a faithful witness to the belief that God has created each person with unique gifts. Those who encourage not only recognize others' God-given gifts but also work to help the gifts blossom in service. As an abbess Saint Hilda required all those in her keeping to devote time to prayer, to the study of the Scriptures, and to doing good works. She knew that a spiritual gift, like a seed in a garden, needed to be tended and nurtured before it could bring forth fruit. Because of her encouragement, many vocations came from Whitby. Her nurture and support led to the full flowering of Caedmon's poetic vocation.

The source of encouragement is a trusting relationship with God. Hilda drew from a lifetime of faith, offering guidance to those in her care. She often offered hope in difficult situations, such as at the Council of Whitby.

Words of encouragement are often very simple. Sometimes we experience them in a gentle invitation or a loving suggestion. Often we remember the exact moment when someone inspired us to step out in faith. To pray with Hilda is to acknowledge the value of encouragement in community, to celebrate its fruitfulness in our own life, and to open ourselves to give and receive encouragement.

- Hilda encourages us to "trade with the gifts God has given you." What gifts do you bring to your dealings, or "trade," with others? Do you use these gifts with the awareness that they are from God?

- Hilda encouraged Caedmon to sing his songs and to join the monastic community so that he would have a strong foundation for his poetry. Picture some people who, at this time, need your encouragement. What words do they need to hear? What means could you provide to help them?

- A word of encouragement often has great power. Recall words of encouragement you have received in the past. Did those words have a lasting effect? How have they influenced your life? Did the person offering the words also offer a means of encouragement?

- Listen to your own words as you speak to others today. Pay attention to the words you say and the actions you take that encourage others. Notice when you withhold encouragement.

- There is often encouragement in the presence of a person of great faith. In such a person, we may apprehend the empowering Spirit; we may take heart in her or his faithful service, particularly in adversity. Do you know someone who encourages you in this way? What gifts are they calling forth in you?

- Listen to Jesus' words of encouragement to his disciples: "Take heart, it is I; do not be afraid" (MATTHEW 14:27). Repeat these words quietly, resting in the assurance of Christ's words to you.

## God's Word

*May the God of steadfastness and encouragement grant you to live in harmony with one another, in accordance with Christ Jesus, so that together you may with one voice glorify the God and Father of our Lord Jesus Christ.*

(ROMANS 15:5–6)

*Closing prayer:* Living God, your presence among us offers hope and encouragement; grant that I may offer those gifts to others, for the life of the world. Amen.

## Meditation 16

# Saint Samthann of Ireland: Praying in All Ways

*Theme:* The holy woman Samthann offers us a life that teaches and models prayer in a variety of ways and in all places. Her deep awareness of God's presence in every moment, in every circumstance, in every place, calls us to a contemplative attitude toward life itself.

*Opening prayer:*

> The Three Who are over me,
> The Three Who are below me,
> The Three Who are above me here,
> The Three Who are above me yonder;
> The Three Who are in the earth,
> The Three Who are in the air,
> The Three Who are in the heaven,
> The Three Who are in the great pouring sea.
> *(Carmina Gadelica,* p. 217)

## About Samthann

The founder of the monastic house of Clonbroney in Ireland in the seventh century, Samthann is remarkable for her wise and moderate counsel. A variety of stories reveal her common sense. She, like Saint Brigit (see Meditation 2), had the gift of soul friendship.

As a young woman, Samthann was betrothed in an arranged marriage by her father. After the ceremony, Samthann prayed that she could be freed from the marriage so that she might become a nun. An amazing flame was seen to come forth from her mouth, a sign of the Holy Spirit's presence. Both her father and her new husband, chastened by the appearance of the flame, recognized her vocation and relinquished their hold on her, allowing her to enter the monastic life.

Samthann later became the foundress of the monastery of Clonbroney. Already known for her teaching and her prayers, Samthann was called because she was clearly inspired and guided by the Holy Spirit. As abbess of Clonbroney, she guided many who sought her wisdom. It was said that her prayer released captives in chains from prison, tamed wild animals, and increased supplies of food.

Samthann understood that the life of faith requires a balance of study and of prayer. A teacher once came to her for advice saying, "I propose to give up study and give myself to prayer." Realizing that for this teacher such a move was not healthy, Samthann counseled, "What then can steady your mind and prevent it from wandering, if you neglect spiritual study?" She recognized that God speaks to us both through prayer and through study, and that both are necessary for a faithful practice of the Christian faith.

This teacher then told her that he wished to make a pilgrimage. Given the teacher's desire to give up study, she seems to have recognized that the desire to go on pilgrimage might be rooted in running away from something. She replied, "If God cannot be found on this side of the sea, by all means let us journey overseas. But since God is near to all those who call on him, we have no need to cross the sea. The kingdom of heaven can be reached from every land." (Sellner, p. 198)

Thus Samthann helped the teacher to see that whatever was awry in the circumstances of his life, he did not need to flee to find God's presence. She gently urged the teacher to allow himself to be taught—to be taught that God is present with us in all times and in all places, filling all things with divine presence.

Samthann lived out her days at Clonbroney, renowned for her counsel and for her charity. As is often the case with the Celtic saints, she is known for her open generosity, both to the sisters of her monastic house and to those who came out of hunger and illness. The sayings and stories we have received about her reveal a woman marked by kindness, wit, and down-to-earth wisdom. Though she participated in a monastic reform movement that was taking hold in Ireland during the seventh century, she was not given to excessive discipline. Hers was a life marked by the recognition of God's presence, a recognition that allowed her to lead others to awaken to awareness of divine presence no matter the circumstances, no matter the place, no matter the time.

*Pause:* When have you been surprised by an awareness of God's presence?

## Samthann's Words

"In every position, a person should pray."

(Sellner, p. 198)

## Reflection

In the Celtic tradition we encounter a keen sense of God with us "in every pass." Samthann's sayings and teachings reflect this. We can make the mistake of thinking God is with us only in church, or only when we are saying a particular prayer, or only when we are engaged in some activity of service. On the contrary, God in Christ reveals to us that there is no place where God is not. Every moment of time, every speck of the universe, is saturated with divine presence. Were that not the case, there would be no time, no space.

Samthann calls us to allow ourselves to become aware of God's presence no matter what position we pray in, whether we are at home or on pilgrimage, whether we are studying or praying. This begins with simply paying attention—paying attention to our lives, to our surroundings, to our friends, to ourselves. This may sound easy. However, in a culture as rushed and harried as ours, paying attention may require more practice that we'd expect! Paying attention happens more easily when we slow down, become aware of our breath, and see what is right in front of us.

Over time, with steady practice of paying attention, our perception shifts. The hidden presence of God begins to make itself known, gently and steadily. When we allow ourselves to step aside from the rushed pace to which we have become accustomed, we begin to see with a loving gaze. As we begin to attend to what is in front of us and what is in our peripheral vision, what our intuitive glance allows us to know, we, like Samthann, will know the question underneath the question. Just as she knew that the teacher's real question seemed to be, "Is God really here with me, in my teaching and in my study, here at home?"—so we come to receive another person's questions or stories with a heart that knows that already Christ is with that person, that already the Holy Trinity has encompassed that person every step of the way.

- Samthann tells us "In every position a person should pray." What position is your body usually in when you pray? Pray as you normally do—kneeling, standing, sitting, lying down. Notice any changes in your breathing or in the muscles in your body. Do you have a sense that your body is participating in the prayer? What does that feel like? Have you ever had the feeling that your body started the prayer before you began to pray consciously?

- One lovely way to pray is with a walking meditation. This is done slowly, gently, accommodating the rhythm of the prayer to the rhythm of the walking. Spend fifteen minutes walking slowly, repeating the following prayer in a way that matches your steps:

  God with me lying down,
  God with me rising up,
  God with me in each ray of light.
  (Carmina Gadelica, p. 6)

  What do you notice about prayer done while walking? How does it differ from your normal prayer?

- Reflect on your usual activities upon waking and getting ready for the day. Note how you begin each morning—do you have an alarm clock? Or do you wake up naturally? Do you shower first thing or get a cup of coffee? Do you walk the dog, feed the cat, water the plants? Make note of how you begin the average day. Then take the time to notice whether you are starting the day with an awareness of God's presence. Remembering Samthann's counsel that we should pray in every position, write some short prayers to go along with your normal activities. These can be as simple as "help" or "thanks".

- Learning to pay attention begins with being still and seeing. Choose one place where you live—a chair, a bench, a couch—a place where you can sit quietly. For the next week, spend ten minutes a day in that place, simply noticing what is there. You might want to make some notes in a journal each day. After you have finished the week, ask yourself how your awareness has shifted. What do you know now that you did not know at the beginning of the week? Create a simple prayer of thanksgiving for a growing ability to pay attention.

- Take a moment to think about the various places you have been in this week—the grocery store, the office, a school, a market. Remembering that "God is near to all those who call on him," note if there was a place in which you felt God to be present. What feelings did that evoke? Note if there was a place where you felt God to be absent. What feelings did that bring? Ask for guidance in seeing God in the places that seem devoid of God's presence.

## God's Word

*I pray that, according to the riches of his glory, [God] may grant that you may be strengthened in your inner being with power through his Spirit, and that Christ may dwell in your hearts through faith, as you are being rooted and grounded in love. I pray that you may have the power to comprehend, with all the saints, what is the breadth and length and height and depth, and to know the love of Christ that surpasses knowledge, so that you may be filled with all the fullness of God.*

(EPHESIANS 3:16–19)

*Closing prayer:* Gracious God, grant me the grace and wisdom to perceive your presence in all places, at all times, within all persons, to the glory of your Name. Amen.

# Meditation 17

# Saint Ciaran
# of Ireland:
# Trust in God

*Theme:* St. Ciaran, one of the "Twelve Apostles of Ireland," a friend to both animals and people alike, founded the great monastic city of Clonmacnoise. He followed the guidance of Saint Enda and the leading of the Holy Spirit in starting the monastery. Trusting in God's call, he began a community of faith and learning. Soon after, Saint Ciaran died of the yellow plague. Nevertheless, Clonmacnoise flourished. The place he had founded, having trusted in the guidance of the Holy Spirit, became a center of learning and devotion for all of Europe. Even though Ciaran did not live to see the full flower of his monastery, he trusted God's guidance to initiate a new community for the love of Christ. Ciaran invites us to trust in God, and to risk new beginnings, even when we may not be present for the full fruition of those beginnings.

*Opening prayer:*

> God's blessing be yours,
> And well may it befall you;
> Christ's blessing be yours,
> And well be you entreated;
> Spirit's blessing be yours,
> And well spend you your lives,
> Each day that you rise up,
> Each night that you lie down.
>
> (*Carmina Gadelica,* p. 68)

## About Ciaran

Among the accounts of Saint Ciaran's life, one finds references to ways in which his life reflected the life of Jesus. Ciaran's father was a carpenter. Ciaran endured the jealousy of others because of his ability to teach, which brought him followers. Ciaran died at the age of thirty-three, having succumbed to the yellow plague in 548, a time known as "the Great Mortality," for many died from this disease.

As is the case with many of the Celtic saints, Saint Ciaran had kind relationships with a variety of animals. He befriended a fox, who carried his Psalter for him. When Ciaran decided to go to Clonard to be with Saint Finnian, he took a dun cow and her calf with him; the cow provided the residents of Clonard with plentiful supplies of milk. A friendly stag allowed Ciaran to place the book he was studying on the deer's antlers, serving as a kind of book rest. The animal companions lead us to see Ciaran as a man who respected and befriended the creatures of God.

Saint Ciaran had a great love of learning, and studied with Saint Finnian of Clonard, among others. The stories of Ciaran's life often have details about the books he carried—a Psalter, a book of gospels, other texts. A literate and learned man, he was not puffed up by his own knowledge and wisdom. Once a fellow scholar in need of a book found, to his dismay, that the other scholars in his community would not lend or give any of their books. However, when he asked Ciaran for a book, the saint immediately relinquished the gospel he was reading. He had just read this verse from Matthew's Gospel: "All those things which you want people to do for you, you also must do for them." Given the opportunity to act as the gospel directed, Ciaran did so. (Sellner, p. 82)

Once when Ciaran went to visit Saint Enda on the island of Aran, both of them had a vision of a great tree growing alongside a river. Enda declared that Ciaran was being called to found a church on the banks of that river. Later, Ciaran journeyed to the banks of the River Shannon, at a place that was a crossroads. One of the main north-south roads of that time crossed the River Shannon. Ciaran founded Clonmacnoise at that spot, in 545, living there just a few years until his death. Yet this "tree" that was the monastery of Clonmacnoise continued to grow and flourish. The seed that he had planted became a great monastic city of learning, a kind of Celtic university, to which people from all over Europe came to study. Saint Ciaran, who believed in handing on what he had received, handed on a life of learning and community. At a time when life on the continent was precarious to say the least, at Clonmacnoise the light of learning continued to burn brightly, thanks to Saint Ciaran's fidelity to the guidance of God.

*Pause:* In what way have you been invited to trust God, not knowing the outcome?

## Ciaran's Words

"Go to meet him who will be your abbot after me."

(Sellner, p. 85)

## Reflection

Ciaran had an awareness of the transitory nature of earthly life. He entrusted himself to God, all the while recognizing that his time on earth was fleeting. He cherished this world as good, and loved the animals as God's own good creatures. He valued his friendships with Enda, Columba, Finnian, and many others. Even in the role of abbot, Ciaran reminded his community that he would not be with them forever, telling them to meet the one who would be his successor. In this, as in other ways, Ciaran's life mirrors the life of Jesus. Ciaran leaves a community formed in faith, a community that is quite young when Ciaran succumbs to the plague. Yet he trusts that the God in whom we live and move and have our being will continue to bless the community that Ciaran has founded in obedience. He desires that the community will thrive and prosper long after he dies. He realizes that his life is like a seed planted in the ground, a seed that must die in order for the plant to come forth. Ciaran helps us to remember both that human life is short and fragile, and to be mindful of the heritage that we leave for those who follow us. He encourages us to think about the generations to come, and to desire to finish our days having left this world a better place than we found it.

- Make a list of five people who have been generous teachers for you. These may or may not be teachers you had in school. They could be wise older relatives or friends, or someone who helped you learn a skill like knitting or gardening, or fellow seekers who have imparted wisdom about the life of faith. Take some time to make your list. Then, beside each name, note what that teacher has handed on to you. Give thanks for the gift, and if possible write a note of gratitude. Then ask yourself if you are handing on what you have received. If not, begin to reflect on how you might do that.

- Who has handed on something precious to you for its nurture and care? How have you responded? Give thanks for the trust you have received, and pray for the continued care that will be needed. This could be the work of a committee, or a communal project, or a familial tradition, or something else. What changes do you feel led to make? To whom would you wish to hand this on? Ask God to guide your discernments and decisions.

- Make an inventory of the books in your house. Choose some that you are ready to give away, and take them to a local library or to an organization that sells books in order to raise funds. Share your books as Saint Ciaran shared his.

- What do you wish to learn at this point in your life? Pick one thing—a skill, a language, a prayer practice. Then begin to make a plan about starting that new learning. As you begin to learn something new, notice how it feels to be a beginner. Pay attention to how you respond to doing something that you have not done before. What lessons are you discovering? How are you aware of God in the vulnerability of new learning?

- Saint Ciaran had many animals who were holy companions. They came to his aid, befriended him, and sometimes imparted wisdom. How have animals been teachers for you? Perhaps a pet, or a wild animal, or an animal you have known through literature has been a holy companion. Reflect on what you have learned, and give thanks for the life of that creature.

## God's Word

*Neither the one who plants nor the one who waters is anything, but only God who gives the growth. The one who plants and the one who waters have a common purpose.*

(1 Corinthians 3:7–8a)

*Closing prayer:* May God who gives the growth guide me to trust in the guidance of the Spirit, and grant me the wisdom to participate in the common purpose, faithful to my part in the mending of this good world. Amen.

# Meditation 18

# Saint Columbanus of Ireland: A Passion for God

*Theme:* Saint Columbanus stands before us as a powerful example of one whose life was filled with a desire and passion for God. In him we see the true flowering of the Great Commission that the Risen Christ gives his followers: "Go therefore and make disciples of all nations, baptizing them in the name of the Father and of the Son and of the Holy Spirit, and teaching them to obey everything that I have commanded you." (MATTHEW 28:19–20a) Through Columbanus, countless lives were influenced by the fire of his passion for God. As an abbot, a scholar, a preacher, and a contemplative, he engaged all his natural and spiritual gifts to send the light of the gospel among the continental people in a crucial time of Western Christianity. Following his inspiration as a gospel bearer, we learn that one's own pilgrimage to God can be an invitation for many other pilgrims.

*Opening prayer:*

> Thanks be to Thee, Holy Father of glory,
> Father kind, ever-loving, ever-powerful,
> Because of all the abundance, favour, and deliverance
> That Thou bestowest upon us in our need.
> Give to us with it the rich gifts of thine hand
> And the joyous blessing of Thy mouth.
>
> In the steep common path of our calling,
> Be it easy or uneasy to our flesh,
> Be it bright or dark for us to follow,
> Thine own perfect guidance be upon us.
> And in each secret thought our minds get to weave
> Be Thou Thyself on our helm and at our sheet.
>
> (*Carmina Gadelica,* p. 41)

## About Columbanus

Columbanus was known for teaching that life is the road to True Life, which is one's eternal home. The beginning of his road was in Leinster, Ireland, in the year 534. While his mother was carrying him in her womb, she had a dream of a great light that extended over all the earth. She knew that this baby yet to be born would be a servant of Christ.

In his earliest years Columbanus manifested that light by his natural charm, his strength of character, and his desire for learning. He also carried with him a secret intuition that he was called to something beyond his knowing. This intuition led him to live at a hermitage of holy and devout women who helped him discern that his calling was to a dedicated life of prayer and study. This choice was not an easy discernment.

Columbanus was gifted with attractive looks and endearing qualities, and it is recorded that many women as well as his mother grieved at his leaving!

Nevertheless he left his birthplace to study with Sinell, a wise man who was known for his knowledge of Scripture. As Columbanus's great passion for learning was nourished, he decided to enter the monastery of Bangor in Wales and study with the famous Abbot Comgall. Living the monastic rule, with its rhythms of solitude and community, he began to see the pattern of God's loving embrace of humanity and creation. His devotion is seen in his commentaries and prayers written about the psalms.

After twenty years of allowing this monastic pattern to shape his soul, Columbanus began to desire to go to distant lands to speak the Good News in the midst of violence and political disarray. Like other wandering saints or "peregrinatios" of his day, Columbanus realized that this desire was also a spiritual quest to come before the loving face of God. He asked permission from his abbot; with twelve fellow pilgrims, they set sail across the English Channel to Brittany.

This was the beginning of many journeys Columbanus and his companions were to make as they established monasteries in Annagray, Luxeuil, Fontaines, and later to the far reaches of Bobbio in the northern part of Italy. They came to lands that were spiritually depleted. The fervor of Columbanus and his fellow monks was said to be like a beacon to those who had no understanding of the true Christian life. Their evangelism was both by word and by example. Living a strict ascetic life, their humility, freedom, and faithfulness attracted many to their communities. Columbanus led the way by preaching, teaching, and practicing his own times of solitude and prayer.

Like many Christian leaders of passion who see the universal scope of the gospel, Columbanus was often thrust into the prophet's role and had to deal with conflict. He was not afraid to speak the truth, as he perceived it, to those in power in Rome and in Burgundy. In 610, he and his monks were banished from the kingdom of Burgundy and sent home to Ireland. In God's providence, however, the ship ran aground, and they journeyed on to what is now Switzerland. Rowing up the Rhine River, he sought to stir up the spirit of his companions with a boat song that gives us a glimpse of the robust and creative light-heartedness of the saint. In the midst of the difficult and dangerous times, he was always encouraging them to sing with all their hearts to continue onward in the name of Christ.

Eventually the wandering pilgrims made it to Bobbio and there at the age of 72, Columbanus died. As the tradition says, there he encountered the place of his resurrection. His last years were spent copying manuscripts and writing sermons. The broad range of his writings as well as his life story, composed by the Monk Jonas three years after his death, reveal Columbanus to be both a scholar and a mystic. He was at home both in the library and in the cave experiencing God's companionship in creation and its creatures. Columbanus "fared well on the road to Life" and when he reached his heavenly home, there were over sixty monasteries founded and influenced by his life and those of his fellow pilgrims.

*Pause:* What part of the gospel stirs a passion and desire in you?

## Columbanus's Words

O Lord, you are yourself that fountain ever and again to be desired, although ever and again to be consumed. Give this water always, Lord Christ, that it may be in us too a fountain of water that lives and springs up to eternal life. I ask for great things, who does not know that. But you, King of Glory, know how to give great things and you have promised great things. Nothing is greater than you yourself, and you have given yourself to us, you gave yourself for us. Therefore we ask you that we may know what we love, for we ask for nothing other than that you should be given to us; for you are our all, our life, our light, our salvation, our food, our drink, our God.

(Davies and Bowie, p. 77)

## Reflection

Columbanus comes to us as a companion who invites us to honor and delight in the hidden passion that God has given each of us. Columbanus's incredible generosity of spirit and creative imagination inspire us to widen our boundaries and trust in the great things that God can do in all times and all places. The authenticity of his passion is that whatever he seeks for himself, he seeks for others. He reminds us that the greatest action we can do or the greatest mission we can accomplish must always be rooted in prayer and contemplation. A true evangelist, Columbanus echoes the psalmist in singing, "Take delight in the Lord, and he shall give you your heart's desire." (PSALM 37:4)

- Columbanus began his pilgrimage with a holy desire. Like other Celtic pilgrims, Columbanus was not so much concerned with outcome as with dedicating himself to that desire and by naming it in prayer. In following this God-given desire, he encountered peace and confidence. Spend a moment in quietness remembering those for whom you wish to pray. You may do this for family and friends or larger

groups and communities around the world. Express your
holy desires for them, and in this longing, be open to
receiving a vision of this happening. Now try to express the
holy desires you have for yourself. Trust that even if your
desire is not fulfilled in the way you see it, God will honor
and bless your desire.

- The Celtic way of evangelism was not so much passing on
  doctrine or belief as sharing the good news one had experienced in one's own life. Reflect for a moment on yourself
  as an evangelist. If someone came to you asking for a word
  of good news, what is one word you could offer? Write that
  word on a card and recall how that word has been experienced in your life.

- Once we become aware of the desires that God has placed
  in our hearts, we need the gift of discernment. Often we live
  out of a passion or desire that is not our own, that is not
  authentic. We discover that our deepest God-given gifts are
  not being lived out in our lives. Begin a list of the gifts and
  abilities that God has given you. Spend some time reflecting
  on how you use your time with these gifts. How do your own
  gifts stir your heart to greater compassion and love?

- The widening circle of a passion for God leads us to transcend the confines of the familiar. As Columbanus says, you
  become "a guest of the world." We are no longer so afraid
  of stepping out and crossing the boundaries of nations,
  cultures, economics, and social settings. Is there a bound-
  ary that you are being called to step across—whether by
  serving at a homeless shelter, teaching in a new setting,
  participating in a mission experience in a foreign culture,

or joining a group for social and political advocacy? As you identify this invitation to widen the circle of your awareness, what fears, emotions, hopes, and dreams do you notice?

## God's Word

How dear to me is your dwelling, O Lord of hosts!*
My soul has a desire and longing for the courts of the Lord;
my heart and my flesh rejoice in the living God.

Happy are they who dwell in your house!*
they will always be praising you.
Happy are the people whose strength is in you!*
whose hearts are set on the pilgrims' way.

(PSALM 84:1, 3–4)

*Closing prayer:* O Lord, you place within our hearts a holy desire for you. It is that desire that is the beginning and ending of our journcy. Stir up our passion for that journey so that in seeking you, we may invite others to share in the richness and power of your loving salvation. Amen.

# Works Cited

Allchin, A. M., *Pennant Melangell: Place of Pilgrimage.* Gwasg Santes Melangell, 1994.

Allchin, A. M., and Esther de Waal, eds. *Daily Readings from Prayers and Praises in the Celtic Tradition.* Springfield, IL: Templegate Publishers, 1987.

Carmichael, Alexander, comp. *Carmina Gadelica: Hymns and Incantations.* Ed. C. J. Moore. Edinburgh, Scotland: Floris Books, 1994.

Davies, Oliver, and Fiona Bowie. *Celtic Christian Spirituality: An Anthology of Medieval and Modern Sources.* New York: Continuum, 1995.

Doble, G. H. *Lives of the Welsh Saints.* Ed. D. Simon Evans. Cardiff, Wales: University of Wales Press, 1971.

Gardner, W. H., comp. *Poems and Prose of Gerard Manley Hopkins.* London: Penguin Books, 1953.

MacDonald, Iain, ed. *Saint Bride.* Edinburgh, Scotland: Floris Books, 1992.

———. *Saint Patrick.* Edinburgh, Scotland: Floris Books, 1992.

Mackey, James P., ed. *An Introduction to Celtic Christianity.* Edinburgh, Scotland: T & T Clark, 1989.

Maitland, Sara, and Wendy Mulford. *Virtuous Magic: Women Saints and Their Meanings.* New York: Continuum Publishing, 1998.

Marsden, John. *The Ilustrated Bede.* Rev. ed. trans. John Gregory. Edinburgh, Scotland: Floris Books, 1996.

Marsh, William Parker, and Christopher Bamford. *Celtic Christianity: Ecology and Holiness.* West Stockbridge, MA: Lindisfarne Press, 1987.

Reith, Martin. *God in Our Midst: Prayers and Devotions from the Celtic Tradition.* London: Triangle, 1989.

Sellner, Edward C. *Wisdom of the Celtic Saints.* Notre Dame, IN: Ave Maria Press, 1993.

Thomas, Patrick. *A Candle in the Darkness: Celtic Spirituality from Wales.* Llandysul, Dyfed, Wales: Gomer Press, 1993.

Van de Weyer, Robert, ed. *Celtic Fire: The Passionate Religious Vision of Ancient Britain and Ireland.* New York: Doubleday, 1990.

Waddell, Helen, trans. *Beasts and Saints.* Grand Rapids, MI: William B. Eerdmans Publishing, 1996.

Ward, Benedicta. *The Spirituality of St. Cuthbert.* Oxford: Sisters of the Love of God, 1992.

# For Further Reading

Cahill, Thomas. *How the Irish Saved Civilization.* New York: Doubleday, 1995.

de Waal, Esther. *The Celtic Way of Prayer.* New York: Doubleday, 1997.

———. *Every Earthly Blessing.* Ann Arbor, MI: Servant Publications, 1991.

Joyce, Timothy. *Celtic Christianity: A Sacred Tradition, a Vision of Hope.* Maryknoll, NY: Orbis Books, 1998.

Meehan, Bridget Mary, and Regina Madonna Oliver. *Praying with Celtic Holy Women.* Jefferson, Missouri: Liguori Press, 2003.

Newell, J. Philip. *Listening to the Heartbeat of God.* Mahwah, NJ: Paulist Press, 1997.

———. *One Foot in Eden.* Mahwah, NJ: Paulist Press, 1998.

———. *The Book of Creation.* Mahwah, NJ: Paulist Press, 1999.

O'Malley, Brendan. *A Celtic Primer: The Complete Celtic Worship Resource and Collection.* Harrisburg, PA: Morehouse Publishing, 2002.

Pemberton, Cintra. *Soulfaring: Celtic Pilgrimage Then and Now.* Harrisburg, PA: Morehouse Publishing, 1999.

Rees, Elizabeth. *Celtic Saints: Passionate Wanderers.* New York, NY: Thames and Hudson, 2000.

Sheldrake, Philip. *Living between the Worlds: Place and Journey in Celtic Spirituality.* Cambridge, MA: Cowley Publications, 1995.

Simpson, Ray. *Exploring Celtic Spirituality: Historic Roots for Our Future.* London: Hodder and Stoughton, 1995.

Skinner, John, trans. *The Confession of Saint Patrick.* New York: Doubleday, 1998.

Woods, Richard J. *The Spirituality of the Celtic Saints.* Maryknoll, NY: Orbis Books, 2000.

Readers interested in guided pilgrimage tours of the Celtic lands
and sacred sites can find further information by contacting

**Hospites Mundi**
51 Laurel Lane
Black Mountain, NC 28711
members.aol.com/HospiMundi/index.html

**Celtic Pilgrimages**
Therese Elias, OSB
Guardian Angels Monastic House
4220 Mercier
Kansas City, MO 64111

Shalem Institute for Spiritual Formation also offers yearly pilgrimages. They may be contacted at:

**Shalem Institute**
5430 Grosvenor Lane, Suite 100
Bethesda, Maryland 20814
www.shalem.org